DRESS to EXPRESS

Dress to Express

Seven Secrets to Overcoming Closet Trauma and Revealing Your Inner Beauty

Tracy McWilliams

New World Library
Novato, California

New World Library
14 Pamaron Way
Novato, California 94949

Copyright © 2004 by Tracy McWilliams

Front cover design by Mary Ann Casler
Text design and typography by Mary Ann Casler

Library of Congress Cataloging-in-Publication Data
McWilliams, Tracy
Dress to express : seven secrets to overcoming closet trauma
and revealing your inner beauty / Tracy McWilliams.
p.   cm.
Includes index.
ISBN 1-57731-452-2 (trade pbk. : alk. paper)
1. Women's clothing—Psychological aspects. 2. Women—
Psychology. 3. Self-esteem in women. 4. Body image in
women. 5. Beauty, Personal. I. Title.
GT1720.M38 2004
391'.2—dc22   2004002972

First Printing, June 2004
ISBN 1-57731-452-2
Printed in Canada on partially recycled, acid-free paper
Distributed to the trade by Publishers Group West

10   9   8   7   6   5   4   3   2

To Goldie,
an amazing woman who knew how to live
in her own power and because of this
touched the lives of so many.

CONTENTS

PART III
Creating the Perfect Clothing Plan

ACKNOWLEDGMENTS

With gratitude to all the people who made this book possible: my husband who provided me with the support and encouragement to continue on this creative path; my mother, Maxine, who has always been there for me with a kind word, an ear to bend, or advice on anything and whose style is all her own; my sister, Sandra, who has a keen sense of how things look together — both she and my mother had the patience to listen to everything related to the book and have provided me with an endless source of friendship; my father, Richard, who has believed and taught me that anything is possible; my brother, Mark, who knew it would all work out; and Lester Boxer for his astute legal advice.

To Georgia Hughes, my editor, who has been a source of encouragement as she guided me through the process of giving birth to a book; her outstanding team included Kevin Bentley and Kristen Cashman. To each person at New World Library who believed in the value of this book and who has had a hand in making it a reality, many thanks.

To my friend Gity Hebel, the owner of Gity Joon's, a unique authentic clothing store on Union Street in San Francisco, who has always believed in me and who has taught me so much about life, friendship, and the ability to create the life I want. To Dean Willis, whose encouragement through this creative process meant a lot. Many thanks to friends and family alike for believing in the power of "I can," and blessings to all!

INTRODUCTION

Starting Within: The Truth about Beauty

I have never known a really chic woman whose appearance was not, in large part, an outward reflection of her inner self.

— Mainbocher

Women love looking good. In our efforts to satisfy this need to look good we may use clothing, jewelry, makeup, hair products, and anything else that can improve our appearance. Many of us also derive satisfaction from inner growth: reading books, attending seminars, doing creative work, and increasing our knowledge and expanding our sense of self. We may not always connect these drives, but both are essential because they create hope for an ideal self.

Clothing and the contemplation of what to wear bring out all sorts of feelings and emotions in every one of us. Sometimes the process of trying to look good can be overwhelming. Knowing what to wear and buy to achieve that aim can leave us feeling like fashion wannabes, or hamsters on treadmills. Often, there is nothing logical or rational about a woman's behavior when it comes to getting dressed or shopping for the right clothes. We just want to look good and feel good about ourselves.

Shopping can give us a kind of rush or high. Buying a new outfit or filling multiple bags with clothing items as we search through the department stores makes us feel good. After shopping, we can't wait to get home and pull our purchases out of the bags to see what we bought. The men in our lives, if there are any at the time, can't understand this process. We may even have to hide our purchases; some women have been known to leave their shopping bags in the car before safely stashing their new clothes in the closet. All of this just so we don't hear the standard male dialogue: "Why did you buy that?" If we do show them a new purchase, they may not be suitably impressed. But we know the right new clothing item can change our look and raise our spirits. Depending on our mood, or the way we feel about our body in the moment, clothes shopping can sometimes create anxiety about the way we look instead of the shopping rush we typically feel.

Why will women go to almost any lengths to look good? We care. We care what other people think of us, we care how we feel about ourselves, we care about making a positive impression for a job or a date or a night out and we care about fitting in or standing out. Sometimes we care too much about what other people think and then we forget to dress for who we are instead of who they are. Concern for our appearance is why we collectively spend billions of dollars annually trying to attain the right image and clothing look. If we have given our self-image some careful thought, shopping and dressing can be fun — and with each new look we can create or connect to a new sense of self.

Shopping for many of us is like an outing to Disneyland. We can't wait to find the perfect, flattering piece of clothing, especially if we are shopping for a special event. Our closets are full of perfect purchases, so much so that many of us experience overwhelming anxiety when we stand in front of the closet trying to choose the right clothes to wear. This anxiety is what I call "closet trauma." Not all of our purchases were perfect, many clothing items were bought on impulse, and some just never fit right. Not knowing what to wear to reflect the real you can result in feelings of closet trauma. These feelings are experienced by all of us, albeit to different degrees and at differing frequency; perhaps only once in a while by some women (not knowing what to wear for that special occasion) but all the time by others (unsure of what to wear every day). This crazy process can be all-consuming and emotionally draining. Not being able to find the right clothes to wear can make us feel bad about ourselves or our bodies. Not knowing what the right kinds of clothes are for us as individuals in the first place can make us feel worse. Deciding what to wear can turn a normal rational woman into a neurotic, self-critical mess. Linda tells us:

> *My husband can attest to my clothing craziness. We have to go out to dinner with some friends so I begin the process of getting dressed. No sooner have I opened my closet door than my heart begins to race and panic sets in. I have no idea what I am going to wear. Now my emotions are kicking in and the inner dialogue begins: "The pants I just tried on make my butt look as if it needs its own zip code, so off they go. Maybe I should just wear a skirt and try to cover it up. What skirts do I have that I like?" By this time the bedroom floor is covered with clothing rejects and to make matters worse, my husband walks back in. His mere presence shocks me into the reality of my clothing desperation.*

What are we really searching for when shopping for clothes or getting dressed? *We are searching for the right outfit or clothing look to make us feel secure in our selves. This feeling of confidence and security comes from knowing that we have maximized our beauty potential and are dressing to show off our greatness.*

When we are experiencing closet trauma we may not feel beautiful. We may feel like a woman in search of herself. When you are feeling the effects of closet trauma, stop and think about what actually makes a woman beautiful. A woman's beauty must first come from the inside. There are five characteristics that highlight a woman's inner beauty:

✦ CONFIDENCE: To be confident is to be in your power as a woman. (This is described in more detail in chapter 4.)

✦ LOVE: A woman who puts out the energy of love or kindness gets it back tenfold.

✦ THE ABILITY TO PUT OTHERS FIRST: A woman who is able to take the focus off herself and direct her attention to the people she is with is beautiful.

- **THE ABILITY TO LISTEN:** When a woman listens to other women or the men in her life, she is captivating.

- **A SENSE OF HUMOR:** Laughter brings out your inner beauty and makes those around you happy.

Embracing these five characteristics helps us to create a level of sanity and awareness. Combined with the five truths below, these characteristics help to give us a sense of personal value, one that comes not just from the way we look on the outside but radiates charismatically from within. Here are five basic truths that can help us to better know who we are and what makes us beautiful:

- **WE ALL HAVE VALUE IN THE WORLD BEYOND THE WAY WE LOOK.**

  Our real value is not based on what we wear or how we look. Our real value comes from the life we create: the person we are, the friends and family members whose lives we touch, and the way we live our lives. What does this have to do with clothing or closet trauma? It's important to understand that if you do not know how great you really are, no outfit in the universe will fix that.

- **HOW WE DRESS AND THE WAY WE LOOK MUST FLOW FROM THE INSIDE OUT.**

  A rose is only a beautiful rose while the rose plant is healthy and happy and receiving water and tender loving care; it's the same for women and the way we dress. The most beautiful women I know radiate beauty from the inside out first. They like themselves and accept who they are. When a woman takes the time to look good, she is confident. With this inner confidence, she is able to turn her attention away from herself to focus on other people and this makes her beautiful.

  Some women who might not meet runway standards of physical beauty are still perceived by those around them as extremely attractive and dynamic. This is because they radiate beauty from the inside out. Imagine how much more beautiful we would all be if we played up our physical attributes with charm instead of working to hide our perceived physical flaws.

To be confident in how you dress is to be comfortable with yourself on the inside. When this occurs a woman's beauty shines forth and everyone notices and wants to be around her. It is beauty not from ego but from a sense of personal worth. A woman who knows her true worth will always be beautiful and charismatic.

✦ WE ARE ALL GODDESSES, MAYBE NOT PERFECTLY PROPORTIONED, BUT EACH OF US IS SPECIAL AND UNIQUE.

How many of us have 36-24-36 measurements? I don't and that's all right because I like my body just the way it is. I do my best to stay healthy and in shape, and still it has taken me years to accept my own body. I think it's more about having learned to accept myself. Like many women, I created tremendous stress in my life for years about the way I looked. I was a size four in my teens and of course I thought I was fat.

When we begin to accept who we are right now, we can enjoy dressing for our particular bodies and expressing our own uniqueness. The women I admire express their own uniqueness in the way they dress and present themselves; they're comfortable not matching what everyone else is wearing. They are comfortable being unique. They put a little extra effort into looking good regardless of body type or weight. They know who they are and are able to express it in the way they dress. Each of us can learn how to dress to express her inner beauty.

✦ WE ARE ALREADY COMPLETE AND WHOLE IN OUR-SELVES, SO NOTHING ELSE CAN COMPLETE US.

We do not need to fix the way we look before allowing ourselves free expression with clothing. We just need to appreciate and enjoy the fact that we have free expression.

We are bombarded with so much information and advertising on what to wear, what's in and what's out, all of it geared to making us feel incomplete, as if we are not enough. If we bought that great jean skirt then we would be enough, if we bought that great leather jacket then we would be enough, if we bought that hot pair of heels then we would be enough, if we bought that sexy see-through T-shirt, then we would be enough — then we would look just like the magazine models, then all of our dreams would come true. So we continue to buy the clothes we see on models, and impulse shop, all the while trying to figure out if we're achieving the look we want and the life we are striving for.

We all have inner beauty that radiates to everyone around us if we allow it. Each of us is simply who we are, and that is what makes us whole and complete. Inner beauty is that something extra that is special to you, a quality no one else has in quite the same way. When we connect to our inner beauty our sense of self-worth shines forth.

✦ THERE IS NO TIME LIKE THE PRESENT TO LET YOUR-SELF SHINE AND EXPRESS THE REAL YOU THROUGH THE CLOTHES YOU WEAR.

The time to be fully who we are, is now. Each day is special and each day requires that we recognize how great we really are. Time passes and we change; this is the natural progression of life. Let change become us, let us enjoy changing and growing into happier, more beautiful people with the following characteristics:

✦ We are excited about the day.

✦ We can't wait to get dressed to show off our inner beauty and creativity.

✦ We put love into the universe because we accept who we and other people are in the moment.

✦ We smile often, especially at the little things.

✦   We appreciate gifts daily, including nature.

✦   We know we are fortunate and we have a strong sense
    of worth.

✦   We let our egos take a backseat because we are already
    whole and don't need them to prop us up.

✦   We enjoy who we are today.

Embracing how fabulous we really are is the key to healing closet trauma and releasing our inner beauty. When we know our true worth, we can learn to dress to express our inner beauty selves.

I wrote this book because I, like so many women, had spent years worrying about what to wear. I wanted the dressing process to be fun and easy, I wanted to be able to snap my fingers and look amazing, and I wanted to be able to feel good about myself and what I chose to wear. The secrets and principles you'll learn in the chapters that follow will help you to do just that. By defining how you want to look, understanding your emotional clothing pattern, and learning how to select the right clothing for your body type, you can banish closet trauma for good and always look great and feel great about yourself.

Blessings on the journey!

PART I

DRESSING FROM THE INSIDE OUT
Seven Secrets for Expressing the Inner You

CHAPTER 1

Define Your Image — and Create One

I have lived in this body all my life and know it better than any fashion designer; I am only willing to purchase the item which becomes me and to wear that which enhances my image of myself to myself.

— Maya Angelou

How you feel and how comfortable you are in the clothes you wear comes from your own self-image. That image is molded by your thoughts as well as your deepest vision of who you are. Confidence is vital to defining that image and creating that vision. Confidence enables you to be comfortable with who you are and how you look. Your confidence level will either support you in selecting the right clothes to wear or create havoc: low self-esteem makes you feel like you can never look good enough. Chapter 3, Claim Your Confidence and Be Lifted Up, explores the importance of confidence to expressing your inner beauty through the way you dress.

The image we create for ourselves directs what is possible for us. Who do you want to be? How do you want to look? How do you want to dress? What do you want people to see when they look at you? Using clothing as a prop, you can give people an immediate sense of you and let your personality shine forth to say, "This is who I am — aren't I great?"

The key to looking great in clothes is understanding that you are the best judge of how you want to look. This is what defining your image is all about. Other people may offer you useful tools for dressing, as this book does, but ultimately, dressing to let your inner self shine forth is what makes you dynamic and beautiful as a woman. Connecting your outer image to your inner beauty is the first step on the journey to clothing bliss.

Clothing bliss is the feeling of calm that is achieved when you are confident that your clothing choices really do reflect your best self. Have you ever noticed someone who is beautifully dressed yet you can sense that she is not comfortable in her clothes or with the image she has created? Perhaps she would like nothing more than to throw off her clothes and put on something else that is more aligned with who she really is inside. On one occasion, I was at dinner with a group of friends and I noticed a woman in the group that I didn't know very well. She was wearing a fitted gold pantsuit with a low-cut burgundy silk top. She spent the whole evening fidgeting in her clothes, pulling her top up because she obviously felt it was too low cut and adjusting her jacket. The out-fit was beautiful and she looked great in it, but she did not feel comfortable and it showed.

If you can dress to express your own personal image, your self-confidence will shine through. In addition, if you can match your clothing image to who you want to be on the inside and carry it off with confidence, you can take yourself further along the path to being the woman you aspire to be. Once you are dressed and out, regardless of where you are going, be confident even if you are not comfortable with your clothing choices because it will show. Dressing your best is about matching your inner beauty with your outer self and vice versa. When the match is complete, looking fab-ulous is the by-product and clothing bliss is the result.

There are three factors that have influenced how we see our-selves and the way we dress today. Some or all of these factors will have played a part in determining our clothing choices up until now:

1. EXPERIENCES: Our past experiences have shaped how we dress and the way see ourselves today. These experiences may be related to family, friends, or strangers. One influence could be something as simple as watching a movie star, see-ing the way the movie star looks, and wanting to follow suit.

Many of us observe movie stars or celebrities and try to copy how they look. We need to remember that they have personal shoppers, image-makers, makeup artists, and personal trainers showering them with attention, and they are usually photographed looking their best.

2. INFLUENCES OF PARENTS, SIBLINGS, AND FRIENDS: Influences related to clothing and image started for most women as children. We learned how to dress from watching our mothers, sisters, or other family members, and later our friends.

If we had strong influences from family and friends growing up, we may have been limited in the development of our own clothing likes and dislikes. For instance, while Sarah was growing up, her mother was a strong force in her life. Sarah was very shy and felt overwhelmed by her mother's strong opinions, especially those related to image and clothing. She would tell Sarah what to wear and what not to wear, according to her own personal likes and dislikes. Yet Sarah and her mother have very different body types: Sarah has a petite frame and her mother is more rounded with a larger bust size. Sarah would end up wearing clothing that would have looked better on her mother, such as long tops or jackets that did not show off her waist. To this day, Sarah still wears baggy sweatshirts and tops in styles that do not highlight her best physical features or true personality. What should she wear? Given her petite frame and small bust, she would be better off wearing fitted tops that show off her small frame. A gathered neckline, a halter top, or a V-neck top are all styles that would work well for Sarah given her small bust. Tops with pockets at the breast line would also be flattering. All of Sarah's clothes should be fitted not too tight or too large; this alone would help to highlight her best physical features.

With their own strong influences such as those Sarah experienced, many women did not learn how to dress based on who they are. Instead they learned to dress based on the preferences and dictates of the people around them.

They weren't permitted to tap into their inner vision of who they are. As adults, many of us continue to make clothing choices based on conditioning and expectations from our childhood.

When we do not develop a strong sense of our own personal image to counteract the clothing and image influences of family and friends, we are likely to find ourselves subject to closet trauma, that out-of-control feeling that comes from not knowing what to wear or how to dress to reflect who we are.

3. OUR INNATE SENSE OF SELF: This is the part of our personality that we cannot easily define; it is our core being. This is the underlying personality we were born with, and through it we develop our likes and dislikes. When this factor is stronger than the two factors above, you experience less closet trauma because you are dressing from your own sense of self relative to image. Our sense of self can become dominant at any point in our lives just through the development and refinement of our own likes and dislikes. When this happens, the two factors above become secondary. In many cases a woman's sense of self may be strong in other areas of her life — in regard to career or relationships — but weak relative to image, clothing, or appearance.

By understanding the factors that have influenced our self-images and the clothing we choose to wear today, we can make choices about our image and appearance that are conscious instead of reactive or unconscious. We can define how we want to look instead of letting the past do that for us. We all have different emotional issues that affect how we feel about ourselves and our appearance; these will be fully explored in chapter 6, Tame Your Clothing Emotions. By dressing today as you would like to be now and in the future, you can develop and improve your image along with your self-esteem.

What if you consciously decided who you wanted to be and then dressed only in accordance with that image? This is how the entertainment business molds its stars. But for most of us, getting dressed has become an unconscious act. We wear the same types and styles of clothing that we have worn for years. Possibly the image we have of ourselves is outdated. Most of us are not even aware of our true preferences and the kind of clothing choices that would make us look the way we have always secretly dreamed of.

We live in a society where other people define us, consciously or unconsciously, by how we appear — and how we dress. Just look at all the advertisers that spend millions of dollars a year telling us how to be beautiful and youthful. Making it possible for others to see us for who we are or want to be helps us build self-confidence and self-esteem.

Do you know what image you are creating? Again, most of us never even think about how we dress. We learn how to dress and unknowingly create a self-image by watching our mother or sister and, as we get older, our friends. Some of us are lucky enough to create our own personal style, but most of us still dress based on what we observed growing up and the influences that surround us every day.

The fastest way to change your image and clothing life is to:

+ figure out who you want to be (through thought);
+ define the image that will match who you want to be (create a vision of the clothing you);
+ step into that role by matching the outer image to your inner vision (take the action to implement your vision).

I call these three steps *The Image Circle.*

1. Defining your image comes from your **thoughts** about who you are.
2. These thoughts create the **vision** of how you want to look and dress.
3. This vision will direct you to take **action**, choosing what to wear.

When we dress based on the influences of other people, we bypass **thought** and **vision** in defining our image to go directly to **action**. This creates closet trauma because we have not thought about what to wear based on the vision of who we are inside.

By defining your image, you create a feeling of wholeness because you complete the image circle: *you think about how you want to look, you create a vision of your clothing self, and finally you take action to make yourself clothing beautiful.*

The true image of who you are comes from within. When you bring your attention inward and decide who you are or want to be, you can change anything. You can craft and then implement a new image by matching the outside with who you are on the inside through the way you dress and present yourself. Whatever thoughts you think about yourself are outwardly reflected whether they are negative or positive — this is why controlling your self-communication style, as described in chapter 7, is so important. The clothing image you have created to this point comes from the vision you have of yourself — your inner vision.

In this chapter and throughout the book there are exercises that serve as guides to help you learn how to dress to express who you are, and how to connect to your inner vision. Take a lined pad of paper or notebook and create for yourself a clothing journal. Use it to complete the exercises and for any additional notes you might want to make about styles or types of clothing you have found that look good on you, or ideas for outfit pairings.

EXERCISE
YOUR MAGIC IMAGE WORDS

Here's a way to find out what image you are currently projecting and what image you would like to create. Write down five magic image words that reflect or describe your current image, then think of five magic image words that reflect the image you would like to create. I call these magic image words because they will magically help you transform your current image into a new image with which you'll be happier.

Most people never think about what sort of image they are creating — they just know that they want to look good. We all can look good in the right clothes on a specific day, but how do you want to look visualized from the inside out? What image do you want to create for yourself?

I was surprised by the outcome of this exercise the first time I tried it. I had not realized that I was creating an image of myself based on who I was ten years ago, and reflecting that image in the way I was dressing and the clothing I was choosing to wear in the present. Back then, I would throw on individual clothing items such as black pants and a T-shirt but never bother to create complete clothing outfits. I did not add accessory items such as jewelry or a scarf. My shirts were more fitted than they needed to be, as in my teenage days, and less tailored than they should have been if I wanted to create a look of casual elegance. I needed to update my image and my clothing look to reflect the woman I had become. Do you need to update your image and clothing look? By doing so, you will increase your self-esteem and change what you think is possible in your life.

Look at my list of magic image words. For me to transform the way I dressed and create clothing bliss, I had to change who I thought I was to who I really was today, or aspired to become. To do this, I had to change my current image into a new image and reflect that in my clothing life.

MY CURRENT IMAGE	NEW IMAGE
Fun	Focused
Attractive	Charismatic
Girlish	Beautiful
Sexy	Confident
Playful	Dynamic

Notice the difference between my current image and my new image. I realized when I looked at my current image that I was not dressing as if I took myself seriously. Until I did this exercise, I hadn't realized how I saw myself and what I was projecting to others. What thoughts have created the vision of you? What image have you created? Who do you really want to be and how do you want to dress to reflect that image?

Take a look at the words you've chosen. How do your current image and the new image of you compare? Are they close or far apart? Are you currently reflecting who you are or not at all? Now just for fun, ask a friend or family member to pick five key words that describe your image. How do these words compare to your current image and your new image? Now that you know the image you want to create for yourself, do you know how to dress to project that image?

MY CURRENT IMAGE	OTHER'S VIEW	NEW IMAGE
Fun	Confident	Focused
Attractive	Sophisticated	Charismatic
Girlish	Beautiful	Beautiful
Sexy	Smart	Confident
Playful	Personable	Dynamic

Notice the difference in how I view myself versus how other people viewed me. Too often we have a difficult time seeing ourselves clearly. People that are close to us can provide positive feedback relative to our image. My new magic image words are surprisingly more aligned with how other people already see me. People that are close to you know your personality and the way you are as a person — whether you are dynamic or confident. Those words don't describe a clothing look; they describe an image of you the person that shines forth in your appearance. Image is not just about what you wear, but also about reflecting your inner beauty in the dressing process through your clothing choices. My clothing choices simply need to catch up with who I am now.

Now that you have a better idea of the image you want to create for yourself, do you know how to go about creating that image? How do you begin to know your own personal style? Personal style adds your own unique touch to the image you want to create. How do you make sure you project who you are on the inside and, most importantly, who you want to become?

EXERCISE
PICTURE YOUR NEW IMAGE

Look through fashion magazines to identify a photograph that reflects the image, as described by your magic image words above, that you would like to create. Tear out that picture. Would you be comfortable with that image?

For my picture, I selected a photograph of a woman in a long cream coat with a cream turtleneck, brown pants, and camel boots. I believe that the woman in this photograph portrays the same image that I would like to create. Now, obviously I would adapt this look to match my own personal style, body type, and colors. For example, because I am petite, in order to match my body type, I would choose a coat that is shorter, ends at the hips, and is more fitted. (See chapter 11, Know Your Body, for identifying and dressing to suit your body type.) I would also wear different earrings than the woman in the photograph. She has a heart-shaped face and wears gold stud earrings. My face is oval, so I would wear hoop earrings to best accentuate my particular facial features. The colors in the photo are the perfect colors for me as described in chapter 10, Color Coordinate Your Wardrobe. They match my skin tone and warm complexion. Even though I am adjusting the image or look to my body specifically, I like the way the clothing and accessory items have been paired in the photograph to create an overall clothing look. That is the secret to creating the perfect image for you: find a look you like, then tailor it to your body type and personal taste.

Dressing is really about creating an image that reflects not only who you are to others but more importantly, who you are to yourself. Too often we dress to please others and fit in, instead of dressing to please ourselves. Remember that uncomfortable feeling of wearing something that may have been trendy and "in," but you didn't feel right wearing it? A clothing style that works for your mother, sibling, or friend does not by default work for you. Does the image you are creating fit who you are and who you want to be in the future? Look at the people you admire. What do their images say about them? Does your personal style match who you are on the inside?

EXERCISE

IDENTIFYING PERSONAL CHARACTERISTICS

Now that you have an idea of the image you want to create to match your inner beauty, take the next step by identifying the personal characteristics that define who you are as an individual. Using your clothing journal, follow these steps to define who you are inside.

STEP 1. Pick five key words that best describe the woman you want to be on the inside. For example: loving, kind, strong.

STEP 2. For each word, write down on a piece of paper "I am first word." For example: "I am loving," "I am kind," "I am generous."

STEP 3. Every morning when you wake up, read your "I ams," to yourself or out loud.

STEP 4. Every day, imagine yourself as the "I ams." See yourself behaving that way now. Picture yourself embodying these characteristics before you go to sleep at night.

STEP 5. Think about how you would behave if you really were the "I ams" you wrote down.

STEP 6. Take at least one action to solidify the "I ams" as the true you. For example, if you wrote down "I am generous," do one thing that day to show your generosity with time or money. Give a gift or help a friend.

STEP 7. Look for opportunities to fulfill your "I ams."

STEP 8. Continue to stay connected to your inner and outer beauty. Feel yourself becoming who you aspire to be.

When you can take the five magic image words that describe your outer image and pair them with the five "I ams" for inner vision, you will truly have defined your image. Before long, you won't be acting it out, you will simply become it. To help you dress for the image of the person you want to be, the next chapter will explain how to define your clothing personality type. With this added dimension, you can implement all the magic words in this chapter to create a perfect clothing look and image for you. That is what I did and my perfect clothing image is below:

FIVE MAGIC IMAGE WORDS (OUTER IMAGE)	FIVE "I AMS" (INNER VISION)
1. Focused	1. I am kind
2. Charismatic	2. I am loving
3. Beautiful	3. I am appreciative
4. Confident	4. I am generous
5. Dynamic	5. I am peaceful

SUMMARY

+ The image we create for ourselves comes from who we believe we are.

+ You are the best judge of how you want to look.

+ Three factors have influenced the way we dress: experiences; parents, siblings, and friends; and an innate sense of self.

+ Create the image you want by taking charge of your image circle: thought, vision, and action.

+ Selecting your five magic image words is the first step to defining the self you want to project.

+ Identifying your personal characteristics completes your defined image of you.

CHAPTER 2

Choose Your Clothing Personality

*Know, first, who you are; and then
adorn yourself accordingly.*

— Epictetus

If you were never properly taught how to dress, how would you know what clothing is right for you? When you purchase clothing or dress yourself from your emotions alone, you may have a tendency to go on remote control. This is what causes closet trauma. How do you begin to take a proactive role in choosing what you like to wear? How do you know what clothing is right for you as an individual? How do you ensure that who you are inside matches the clothes you wear on the outside? The Simple Principles for Conscious Dressing in part II provide a how-to of what to wear. The Seven Secrets for Expressing the Inner You will help you to determine on a more fundamental level how you want to look.

I have identified seven steps to the process of choosing how you want to look. These steps help you form a vision of yourself so that you may identify what to wear based on that vision:

STEP 1. Understand the factors that have created the way you look and dress today. These three factors, described in the previous chapter, are (1) experiences, (2) influences of other people, and (3) an innate sense of self.

STEP 2. Consciously choose to dress from an inner sense of self instead of from your emotions. Allow your true personality to shine forth unabated from your own sense of self. Choose to dress for you and then be committed to the choice.

STEP 3. Choose how you want to look based on who you are inside and reflect that person through the image you create. Use your magic image words from the previous chapter to get you started.

When you make a conscious effort to choose the way you want to look by defining your image, the dressing process becomes fun. The image you choose, in part, comes from matching your personality to your clothing choices. This is what creates a clothing personality type.

STEP 4. Know the six clothing personality types. Look at the description of each type below to determine which type you have been. See if you can match your image to a personality type. Each personality type describes how you dress and the image you project. Each provides a simplified version of how you see yourself from the inside aligned with the way you want to look on the outside.

STEP 5. If the clothing personality type matches how you would like to dress and your magic image words selected in the previous chapter, then learn how to dress based on that type, using the principles of conscious dressing in part II and let your inner beauty shine forth.

STEP 6. If the clothing personality type you have been dressing for does not match how you want to look or your new magic image words, choose a more appropriate personality type.

When we don't allow our inner personality to match how we dress, we feel frustrated with the clothing selection process. This is because we have let the influences of other people dictate our clothing personality type. For example, say you have been dressing in clothing that is loose fitting and flowing, in comfortable fabrics such as cotton and linen, because this is what you saw growing up and it is what you know. But maybe you feel that this style of dressing doesn't really fit who you are inside anymore or properly show off your body type. You are ready for a change. Maybe you are drawn to colors and clothing that show off your hourglass shape such as wrap tops that highlight your waist. You enjoy being noticed and like to stand out. As we'll see in what follows, this description is more in line with an Actress personality type than the Artist Type that you have been dressing to express. To more closely fit your personality and bring out your inner beauty, you may want to change your clothing personality type.

STEP 7. Allow yourself creative freedom and make the effort to add spark to your own clothing personality type by selecting unique clothing and accessory items that fit you. If you are a stickler for perfect grooming and love designer items, then as the Socialite Type you may select a Gucci handbag to complete your evening-out clothing look. Know that as you become more aware of your likes and dislikes, you can change how you look in a moment just by making different clothing and image choices.

You do not have to fit one clothing personality type perfectly. With so many clothing styles available today, you have the creative freedom to express who you are and how you are feeling in the moment. The clothing personality types are not simply a way of dressing but truly reflect the person you are. If you like to be casual and comfortable in easy to wear fabrics, you may fit either the Sporty Type or the Artist Type. If you love shopping for clothing and the whole image process, which may include styled hair and full makeup, and you don't mind standing out or being noticed, you may fit the Socialite Type or the Actress Type. If you like the dressing process to be easy, and being classically dressed is a priority for you, then the Classic Type may fit who you are. Finally, if you rebel against the whole dressing process to create your own look, you may fit the Rebel Type. The clothing personality types should serve merely as an outline for dressing to express who you are, rather than a required plan. You may well be a combination of the clothing personality types. The key is to define who you are, what you want your look to express, and what you are comfortable wearing.

As part of describing the six personality types, I have included names of designers and clothing stores that serve as a basis to more thoroughly differentiate the personality types. The clothing stores that you shop in and the designer styles you select may or may not be included. The design of clothing items you select should be based on your own preferences and most importantly how a specific designer's clothing items flatter your body type and fit who you are inside. Because there are so many great clothing designers and clothing stores that offer unique designs, they could not all be included here. Use your clothing journal to note stores and designers whose clothes make you look and feel your best.

Following are the six clothing personality types:

THE SOCIALITE. *I am about image.* I want to appear a certain way. I am always beautifully dressed in designer clothing no matter where I am going, whether just running errands or attending a dinner party. Perfect grooming is a must. My mottos are "I must look my best at all times" and "How I look influences how I am treated." Ivana Trump, Joan Rivers, and Nancy Reagan fit this type.

THE ACTRESS. *I am about standing out.* I am outgoing and creative. I love to be the center of attention. I am attention-getting. I love anything that is in fashion, although my clothing does not have to be, so long as I can tailor the look to fit me and my personality. My mottos are "I love attention" and "I have to stand out." Victoria Beckman, Paris Hilton, Pamela Anderson, and Halle Berry fit this style.

THE CLASSIC TYPE. *I am about chic simplicity.* Less flash is what I prefer. I want to always be appropriately dressed so that I can go anywhere and do anything. My clothing lasts the test of time because it is not trendy. My mottos are "I look classy" and "I am simple elegance." Nicole Kidman, Diane Sawyer, Vanessa Williams, and Maria Shriver fit this type.

THE ARTIST TYPE. *I am about creative comfort.* I like to wear comfortable and flowing clothing in quality fabrics. My style tends to be less fitted, with a casual comfort and a bohemian flair. My motto is "I love comfortable fabrics" or "I love clothing that looks like art." Whoopi Goldberg, Meryl Streep, and Stevie Nicks are good examples.

THE SPORTY TYPE. *I am about being sporty and casual.* I dress in easygoing, down-to-earth fashion. I love to be able to get up and go fast and easy and don't want to spend a lot of time on perfect grooming. My mottoes are "I love to be comfortable" and "My style is preppy casual." Katie Holmes, Calista Flockhart, and Serena Williams fit this type.

THE REBEL. *I am about resisting the establishment.* I will wear whatever I please. I am my own person. Nothing has to match perfectly — in fact I prefer that it doesn't. I create my own look. My mottos are "I will wear whatever I want" and "I don't care what you think." Courtney Love, Angelina Jolie, Lil' Kim, and Pink fit this type.

Your clothing personality type determines to a great degree how you want to look in clothes. Pick your type and then go about building a wardrobe that matches it. Next we'll look at each clothing personality type in detail.

THE SOCIALITE

The Socialite is about image, proper dressing, and fine grooming. She is always crafting an image that will make her appear perfectly dressed wherever she is going. Flawlessly styled hair and makeup are a way of life for the Socialite. She buys the most beautiful and expensive clothes regardless of her financial situation, even if she can only afford one designer piece per season. If money is no object, you will find her in anything couture and top-of-the-line accessory items such as a Hermès Kelly bag. It's all about quality for the Socialite. She believes that what she wears defines her and because of this she always takes the utmost care of her clothing. Clothing is not just a purchase; it is a way of life. Socialites care what other people think of them and are very aware of what other women are wearing. Accessories such as handbags are a wardrobe staple. Clothing items are perfectly tailored and come from top name designers including Chanel, Givenchy, Valentino, Oscar de la Renta, Emanuel Ungaro, Lanvin, and J. Mendel, to name but a few.

The Socialite's Emotional You

"I care a great deal about my image. I love to look as if I can afford the best. It sends a statement that I am worth it. I take the time and make the effort to be attractive. I am defined by what I wear and how I present myself. I believe in the whole image, makeup, hairstyle, and clothing." Most Socialites are strong women whose self-esteem is tied to the fact that they know how they want to look and who they are. Socialites are willing to spend time on their personal image daily because they know it will pay off in major dividends. They set their own extremely high standards for image. Women who are Socialites choose this personality; they don't just fall into it. It takes time and effort to craft the perfect image. Socialites make a significant investment in their wardrobe regardless of their financial situation and they feel it is worth it.

The Socialite's Story

Kelly is a classic Socialite; she is all about image. She takes the time to style her hair and apply her makeup, and then dresses impeccably. Kelly is a Beverly Hills real estate agent who is also on the board of a charitable foundation that helps children. She believes that her image has helped to get her where she is today. You can find her on most days having lunch with clients or potential donors or by herself at a high-end Beverly Hills restaurant. She is usually wearing a well-known designer pant or skirt suit, perhaps a pink and white Escada pantsuit, and of course a designer handbag — Louis Vuitton, Gucci, Chanel, or Hermès. Her hair and makeup are perfect. She makes the effort to craft just the right image because she believes how she dresses affects the way she is treated.

Dressing the Socialite

+ Ultra-casual: Marc Jacobs sundress with strappy flats or Diane von Furstenberg wrap top with Paper Denim jeans and Gucci bag.

+ Casual: white slacks, pink fitted cashmere sweater, ballet shoes, and Hermes Kelly bag.

+ More than Casual: Emanuel Ungaro pantsuit with beaded top and fifties-inspired heels.

+ Dressy: Chanel black and white skirt suit, several pearl necklaces of varying lengths, pumps, nylons, and black Chanel bag.

+ Black-Tie: Brown halter beaded dress, Valentino satin frame bag with feathers, and Jimmy Choo beaded ankle-strap heels.

How to Become the Socialite Personality:

+ Make grooming a top priority. Never leave the house with out your hair and makeup done.

+ Familiarize yourself with the top couture clothing designers and their lines.

+ Know the fashion seasons and the latest designer styles.

+ Decide what couture designer clothing you would most like to wear.

+ Know the image you are interested in crafting.

+ Make sure all your clothing is appropriately taken care of, and hemlines are altered as needed.

+ Be willing to spend money on quality items.

+ Understand that your wardrobe is less about quantity and more about spending for quality.

Are you a Socialite? Are you willing to take time to craft your image? Are you willing to maintain the look long-term? Are you willing to buy designer labels? Do you believe clothing is an investment? Do you believe clothing defines you? If you answered yes to at least three of the above questions you may be a Socialite.

THE ACTRESS

The Actress loves to stand out and is comfortable showing off her appearance. She knows what is in style, yet buys anything that can make her look great, designer label or no. She shops for clothing that highlights her physical attributes: fitted tops, low-rise jeans, pencil skirts, sexy blouses, and short dresses. She is comfortable with the attention she gets from dressing in colors or tighter-fitting clothes. The Actress is less about perfect grooming (Socialite) and more about being fun and flirty. She may or may not have her hair styled on any given day, sometimes preferring to wear it up in a messy ponytail. She knows how to mix and match color, fabric texture, and style for a standout look. You may see her in Manolo Blahnik heels with jeans and a silk flowered top for a day out with friends or dressing as simply as in a Juicy Couture sweat suit with "juicy" printed on the behind, with hoop earrings and sandals. The Actress is dramatic and flamboyant in a hip way. She doesn't have to look perfect, just creative. Versace, Dolce & Gabbana, Chloé, Stella McCartney, Missoni, Christian Dior, and Roberto Cavalli provide standout clothing styles the Actress Type wears.

The Actress's Emotional You

"I love to dress to show me. I care less about molding my image (Socialite) than looking great, having fun, and being playful with clothing. It is in my nature to be outgoing. I feel very comfortable showing off my physical assets in a fun way but never going too over the top (Rebel). I like to spend money not just on the most expensive clothes but on anything that will show off my beauty self." The common factor among Actress Types is that they love standing out in a girlie sort of way or grabbing attention. They have confidence and that allows them to choose bold styles to wear. Actresses can be somewhat self-critical, noticing personal imperfections that no one else sees. They want to look good for their audience and are always looking to improve.

The Actress's Story

Tara is a classic Actress; she wears clothing that fits her body perfectly and knows how to show off her best physical assets. She owns her own cosmetic company and is also one of her own best customers. She is always trying to improve herself, changing her hair color constantly or having a nip and tuck (cosmetic surgery) here or there. On most days you can find Tara in fitted pants or jeans with uniquely cut top styles, a long sleeve T-shirt with the shoulders cut out, for example, or a fitted cashmere V-neck sweater in pink with high heels (her favorite type of shoe) or sexy high-heeled boots. People love Tara because she is her own person — friendly, outgoing, and fun. She is extremely creative and she shows this creativity in the clothing styles and colors she selects. Some days she goes all out to be the funky girlie-girl in a miniskirt with a scalloped hemline, turtleneck, and cowboy boots, which just shows she can mix up style to create her own look.

Dressing the Actress

+ Ultra-casual: Juicy Couture sweat suit with Ugg boots.

+ Casual: tight, low-rise, dark Seven denim jeans; Bebe black bandeau top, white knit scarf wrapped around the neck, red cowboy boots, and gold hoop earrings.

+ More than Casual: red and white striped Dolce & Gabbana pencil skirt; off the shoulder, black, cashmere sweater top; sling back high heels with bow, and retro bag.

+ Dressy: satin black tank top with a green and gold hand-beaded skirt, fitted with the hemline falling just above the knee; gold heels with ankle strap; black antique beaded earrings and a gold beaded clutch.

+ Black-Tie: peach and black, pleated, Stella McCartney chiffon strapless dress with lace hemline falling just below the knee; Manolo Blahnik peach heels with sexy ankle straps, black dangling earrings, and silk wrap.

How to Become the Actress Personality:

+ Be comfortable standing out.

+ Wear clothing items that fit your body perfectly.

+ Be willing to use clothing to highlight your best physical attributes.

+ Be open to improving your physical characteristics every chance you get.

+ Add creative flair to everything you wear.

+ Always look for unusual clothing items and accessories in unique fabrics or styles that can show off your creative flair and body in a fun, flirty way.

+ Learn to mix and match fabrics, textures, and styles.

+ Be extroverted; let your personality shine through in what you wear.

Are you an Actress? Do you love to stand out? Do you love getting attention? Are you focused on your beauty self all the time? Are you outgoing? Are you always trying to improve your looks? If you answered yes to at least three of the above questions, you may be an Actress.

THE CLASSIC TYPE

The Classic Type is always appropriately dressed. She loves dressing for the occasion and enjoys wearing classic tailored clothing items that fit her body type but are not flashy. Black is a staple in her wardrobe and the clothes she chooses have classic, simple lines. She wears a limited amount of accessories but the accessories that she does wear add a touch of flair and style to her outfit; a Hermès scarf with a black sheath dress is a perfect example. She can dress in a suit for any occasion, simply altering the look by changing her blouse, shoes, and accessories to fit the event. A suit with a turtleneck and pumps is perfect for the office; by changing into a camisole and open-toed heels, she's ready for an evening date. The Classic Type likes simple clothing styles that get her noticed instead of just her clothing. A fitted pantsuit, a black dress, a turtleneck, a trench coat, and pumps are wardrobe must-haves for a Classic Type. Styles from Calvin Klein, Armani, and Prada fit the Classic Type personality.

The Classic Type's Emotional You

"I love to look good and classic in the way I dress. I know who I am and do not have to be flashy to show it. My confidence always shines through. I admired Jacqueline Kennedy Onassis and the way she dressed. She was classic in her beauty and dressed as if less were more. I like my clothing to highlight me and be conservatively stated." Classic Types are not about wearing the most expensive items (Socialite) or standing out and showing off their best physical assets (Actress). They want to be admired for their classic beauty and taste. They feel attractive and don't have to gild the lily. The clothing styles for the Classic Type are never out of style but never really in style — they are just classic and stand the test of time.

The Classic Type's Story

Lynn is the Classic Type. She is a corporate lawyer and always has to be appropriately dressed on short notice, whether the occasion is a client meeting, an office party, or a date. In her closet you will find lots of black items, simple dresses, and suits with clean lines. She feels that she will never be over- or underdressed in whatever she wears. For an office party Lynn wore black Calvin Klein slacks and a button-down black silk blouse, with a beautifully patterned Burberry wrap around her shoulders and black sling back shoes to finish her outfit. Her earrings were diamond studs. After her office party she met some girlfriends for a night on the town wearing the same suit but changing into a lace top and sexy heels.

Dressing the Classic Type

+ Ultra-casual: jeans, white button-down shirt, red sweater tossed over the shoulders, and flats.

+ Casual: black pants, pink sweater, scarf around the neck, and slip-on kitten heels with trench coat.

+ More than Casual: black and white A-line skirt, Banana Republic white crisp button-down blouse with black cardigan over it, black riding boots, and red Italian leather satchel.

+ Dressy: navy Calvin Klein classic pantsuit, sheer mesh crewneck top with pearls, navy stiletto pumps, and a Louis Vuitton Sorbonne handbag.

+ Black-Tie: sleeveless and low back Valentino halter dress with long hemline to the ground, black open-toed heels, dangling rhinestone earrings, vintage beaded clutch, and velvet wrap.

How to Become the Classic Type Personality:

+ Dress to be understated but classy.

+ Know how to be appropriately dressed for every occasion.

+ Choose muted or dark colors that allow you to look good but fit in as well.

+ Buy clothing items that make complete outfits and stand the test of time, such as suits or simple dresses.

+ Buy accessories that match the classy look and blend with your wardrobe, such as scarves.

+ Let your personality shine through and be the focal point, rather than bright colors or unusual clothing items.

Are you the Classic Type? Do you like clean, simple clothing that is beautifully tailored? Do you own a lot of black? Are you relatively conservative in your dress? Do you like your personality to shine through? If you answered yes to at least three of the above questions you may be a Classic Type.

THE ARTIST

The Artist wears fabrics her body loves — comfy cottons, for example. There are many clothing styles for the Artist. You are an Artist Type if you prefer (1) casual cotton or linen outfits with earthy tones or neutral colors that are loose fitting; (2) more of a "gypsy" look, such as a long-tiered skirt and a cotton scrunched blouse with long sleeves, in vibrant colors and unique embroidery; or (3) the romantic free-flowing look, for instance, chiffon halter tops with flowing matching skirt. You can be one of these three clothing styles without having to fit the other two. The Artist dresses for comfort and creativity, with less focus on dressing for her particular body type. Unlike the Sporty Type (see below) the Artist is not about preppy casual but more about bohemian style. The Artist may wear drawstring pants and a button-down top with no collar in off-white silk fabric, or go to the other extreme of offbeat fabrics such as patchwork or hand-knitted items. For the Artist Type described in item (2) above, creativity comes out in clothing that appears more like art, such as items that have fringes or embroidery and hand-painted dresses in cotton or silk. Eskander, Eileen Fisher, and Donna Karan New York are designers the Artist might wear, as well as some styles from Elie Saab.

The Artist's Emotional You

"I like to be comfortable in the clothing I wear, nothing too tight. I like being dressed in an easy, relaxed manner. I don't believe I have to be flashy or obsessed with fashion. Of course I like to look good, but that does not necessarily define me. Flowing, casual comfort would be how I describe my clothing image and look. Fashion is about connecting to me. I love to be able to throw on clothes that are interesting and comfortable and go out. I can pair a long white linen skirt with a cotton, hand-painted blouse and a drawstring satchel bag for a complete outfit." Depending on the category you fall into in the Artist Type, you are likely to be one of two extremes: you like the subtlety of your clothing look, muted colors, earthy tones, drawstring pants in beige with a long camel-colored top over them, for example; or you like your clothes to look artsy with color in either handmade fabrics or flowing pastels.

The Artist's Story

Anne is the Artist Type; she is an archaeologist and loves to wear comfy, free-flowing fabric that gives her ease of movement. She loves to travel, which she does a lot of in her work, and likes to get dressed simply to be comfortable in a relaxed manner and of course look good. She isn't interested in flash (Actress) or fitting in (Classic); she is interested in showing off who she is through her unique choice of clothing. She fits the Artist Type in category 1 above, favoring casual linen, cotton, or silk wear in loose-fitting fabrics.

Dressing the Artist

+ Ultra-casual: red cotton gauze pants, light beige long-sleeve crewneck shirt, beige and red patchwork bag, red sandals, and red knit hat.

+ Casual: blue Indian sari wrap with beading, black sandals, and funky blue earrings.

+ More than Casual: white linen pantsuit; black and white polka-dot, ruffled, sleeveless blouse; fringe pouch; slip-on heels.

+ Dressy: gold and red silk flower-patterned pants, red velvet corset, gold brocade jacket, beaded satin heels with gold dangling earrings, and red and gold inlaid clutch.

+ Black-Tie: silk and velvet pink top with an empire waist; black vintage belt and long, tiered black chiffon skirt; black and pink silk shawl; crystal earrings; peephole pink pumps; and black wrist-strap clutch.

How to Become the Artist Personality:

+ Dress to be casual and relaxed.

+ Choose clothing with fabrics that are natural and feel great against the body — cotton and silk, for example.

+ Make getting dressed easy by either matching simple color tones or, on the other extreme, lots of color in your entire outfit.

Are you the Artist Type? Do you like wearing casual, comfortable flowing fabrics? Are you more about wearing unusual designs in fabrics that are comfortable rather than tight fitting? Do you like to buy items that are artistic in nature, meaning the clothing you purchase looks like art? Do you like to show your personality through your clothing choices? If you answered yes to at least three of the above questions, you may be the Artist Type.

THE SPORTY TYPE

The Sporty Type is about preppy casual. She likes simple clothing that is easy to wear and comfortable. Jean jackets; khaki pants; T-shirts; knit sweaters, scarves, and hats; and sportswear are the Sporty Type's clothing choices. Like the Artist, she likes comfortable fabrics such as cotton, her fabric of choice, but unlike the Artist the Sporty Type wears clothing that is fitted and more likely to be suited to her body type. For work, to keep her casual style she might wear something like fitted cotton pants with heels, a striped boatneck top, and a short boxy jacket. She also loves sweat outfits from sportswear makers such as Adidas, Puma, or Nike. She wants a casual, sporty look where the dressing process is easy. J. Crew, Gap, Ralph Lauren, and Tommy Hilfiger are designers and brands the Sporty Type might choose.

The Sporty Type's Emotional You

"I live a casual, sporty lifestyle. I like comfortable clothes that fit well and allow me to run around without putting a lot of effort into what I wear every day." The Sporty Type dresses in a youthful way, with simple, fun accessories such as a wool scarf or a knit hat. A messenger bag may be the handbag of choice, with the strap flung over the body and across the chest. She likes to wear simple, comfortable clothes that are easy to take care of without a lot of dry cleaning. Her wardrobe is full of khakis and cargo pants. The Sporty Type may be an athlete who wears sportswear while participating in outdoor activities like biking and running.

The Sporty Type's Story

Karen loves to dress preppy casual. She throws on a pair of military chino pants and a polo shirt or hoodie, jean jacket, red scarf, and sandals to meet friends for lunch. She works for an Internet-based company where the office dress is casual on most days. This is perfect for her personality because she likes to get dressed without a lot of drama all the time. The need to dress up or look more than casual creates some anxiety for the Sporty Type. When she needs to be more than casual, Karen may be seen wearing a tweed skirt and a long sleeve knit turtleneck with boots. She loves to look well dressed but as if she didn't spend too much time getting that way.

Dressing the Sporty Type

+ Ultra-casual: Gap jeans, flip-flops, tank top with a sweatshirt.

+ Casual: J. Crew army-green chinos; gray, long sleeve crewneck tee with a red, short sleeve Express crewneck tee over it; sandals; and a straw bag.

+ More than Casual: wool brown trousers with Arden B. paisley-patterned empire waist top, wool blazer, and ankle boots.

+ Dressy: black stretch satin pencil skirt, peach silk shell, leather envelope clutch, multiple faux pearl necklaces, black stiletto pumps.

+ Black-Tie: long, black, fitted satin dress with matching neck scarf; dangling earrings; and black platform heels with ankle straps.

How to Become the Sporty Type Personality:

+ Cotton fabrics and knits are wardrobe must-haves.

+ Sweaters, T-shirts, comfy flat shoes such as loafers, khakis, knit hats and scarves, and down vests are what you should wear.

+ Show less skin than, say, the Actress Type.

+ Match jeans with every kind and color of T-shirt; layering T-shirts is definitely a way of life for the Sporty Type.

+ Throw on polo shirts and hoodies with chinos.

+ Clothes should be comfortable and somewhat fitted, but not overly so.

Are you a Sporty Type? Do you like to spend as little time as possible getting dressed and primping? Do you love comfortable fabrics such as cotton? Would you rather be comfy and casual than stand out or always have to think about creating an image? Are other activities more of a priority than shopping? If you answered yes to at least three of the above questions, you may be the Sporty Type.

THE REBEL

The Rebel likes to rebel against the fashion establishment. She wears whatever she pleases. She does not try to be appropriately dressed like the Classic Type or stand out like the Actress. The Rebel is more about making the statement that she can be whoever she wants to be. She wears a lot of accessories, and is likely to have more than the usual piercings (lip, eyebrow, nose, belly). She loves shock value. Any style will work for this woman as long as it is her own. She may or may not choose to wear designer clothing, but if she does she creates her own look with it. A famous pop star, for example, once wore a Christian Dior dress that looked like a torn-up magazine, and two necklaces of different lengths with crosses on them, and her hair, of course, was dyed hot pink.

The Rebel's Emotional You

"I am my own person and I don't care what you think of me. Fitting in is about conforming to the establishment; that's not me. I have friends who accept me for who I am." Rebels are independent truth-seekers. They dress to be real. They dress to create a personalized image of who they are or to create a persona that does not fit any set image category. They like to pair clothing of different looks and styles that no one else would ever put together. Their image is uniquely their own.

The Rebel's Story

Sidney is a rebel and a musician. Her music is all about rocking the establishment through lyrics that are anti-organized anything, whether it be government, religion, or politics. She wears black jeans and T-shirts as her casual look and when she is performing any clothing look goes, including ripped shirts, short skirts with ripped tights, or a designer dress with her added personalized touch — lots of necklaces and combat boots. Her style is her own. She has piercings on her lip and one eyebrow. People like her because she is willing to be her own person and make a statement.

Dressing the Rebel

+ Ultra-casual: jeans; very, very low cut, long sleeve, gray and pink cashmere hoodie with black bra showing underneath; black oversized ornate costume necklace with matching spiked wristband; and punk hair.

+ Casual: black denim skirt with fishnet stockings, stretch tank top, chain belt around the waist, bomber jacket, and ankle boots.

+ More than Casual: black low-rise ankle pants, Bebe seethrough mesh top with black bra, cowboy hat, and low heels.

+ Dressy: pencil skirt, ripped silk top off the shoulder, messy hair, Giuseppe Zanotti Design shoe with a rhinestone snake wrapped around the ankle, and lots of jewelry: twenty bracelets, ten necklaces, and many ear piercings.

+ Black-Tie: colorful Christian Dior dress with spaghetti straps, heels with leather ankle straps, and lots of necklaces and chains around the neck.

How to Become the Rebel Personality:

+ Create your own clothing style.

+ Do not follow the fashion trends.

+ Pair clothing and accessory items that would normally never be seen together.

+ Be willing to go all out to make a statement and rebel against styles that have been widely advertised.

+ Be willing to be noticed and looked at by other less adventuresome people.

+ Have a "this is who I am" attitude.

+ Be interested in wearing anything just for the shock value.

Are you a Rebel? Do you follow your own path? Are you somewhat antiestablishment? Do you have piercing in several spots? Do you wear a lot of black as your clothing style? If you answered yes to at least three of the above questions, you may be a Rebel.

The table below summarizes the six different personality types:

PERSONALITY TYPE	I AM ABOUT	MOTTO	WARDROBE MUST-HAVES
The Socialite	image	"I must look my best at all times."	designer handbag
The Actress	being memorable	"I have to stand out."	pink cashmere V-neck sweater
The Artist	creative comfort	"I have to be me."	beige linen pants
The Classic	simple elegance	"I am always appropriately dressed."	black sheath dress
The Sporty	preppy, easy comfort	"I love to be comfortable."	khaki pants
The Rebel	antiestablishment	"I will wear what I want."	pierced accessories

The designers and clothing stores listed under each of the personality types above make clothing styles that also fit the other listed personality types. For example, Banana Republic's clothing is a combination of styles that fit the Sporty Type and the Classic Type, while the Actress Type may wear their silk V-neck camisoles and other items. I have made generalizations about the clothing styles of the designers mentioned in this chapter and throughout the book, and clearly each personality type may choose to purchase any of the clothing made by any of the designers or clothing stores mentioned.

Most designers, depending on the fashion season, make many different styles and types of clothing. Some, on the other hand, stay with the style of clothing that they have been designing and manufacturing for years, for instance, Armani or Calvin Klein, whose designs are considered classic and therefore work very well for the Classic Type. The clothing store Gap provides items perfect for the Sporty Type, although other personality types may also like to wear their clothes, especially their tank tops and T-shirts, which are wardrobe staples.

In identifying your clothing personality type, keep in mind that there are no hard and fast rules for designers relative to personality type. As stated above, some designers have always manufactured certain lines and styles that change very little. You can always depend on Versace to deliver something that the Actress Type can wear. Versace is known for colors and standout styles that go well with the personality of an Actress Type, but there may also be Versace items that work for the Socialite or other personality types. Some clothing stores offer fun, fashionable clothing with specific items that would fit many of the personality types listed. These stores and brands do create unique clothing looks but may also tailor some of their clothes after those seen on the fashion runways from other more expensive high-end designers. Know what your clothing budget is and know what you are willing to spend on clothing and accessory items. Use the listed personality types as a base to build your own wardrobe choices on. As stated previously, choose clothing styles that work for you from stores or designers whose look reflects you and fits your body type and personality.

When evaluating the clothing personality types, remember that it takes effort if you want to change your current look to a new personality type. For example, some women are the Sporty Type but aspire to be the Actress Type. In order to make this change, the Sporty Type has to be willing to spend a lot more time on clothing creativity and shopping, which may impact her lifestyle. She would also have to become more comfortable with standing out and possibly being the center of attention, instead of being casual and less visible. Know what you are willing to do and understand your comfort level.

You may be a combination of the personality types or need to create your own, using the aspects of the ones I've outlined that fit your own image. For example, a combination of an Actress and the Classic personality type is a woman that likes to stand out but may use classic styles to do so, such as a black gown with a low V-neck front to highlight the bust line. A combination of a Socialite and a Classic Type is a woman who is always crafting her image and who at times wears designer clothing items and accessories in classic styles. Barbara Walters would fit this combination. Jennifer Aniston fits the Classic and Sporty Type combination. At parties or award ceremonies she is usually classically dressed and then on her off time is seen wearing Sporty Type clothing. She has even said that she is a fan of these types of clothes. Oprah Winfrey is very much the Classic Type but also at times fits into the Sporty Type.

This chapter is all about crafting your own look; these personality types can help you to begin to do that.

Benefits to Understanding the Differing Personality Types

✦ You gain insight into why you dress the way you do.

✦ You can learn to evaluate your personality so that you may match who you are inside to the way you want to look and dress on the outside.

✦ In learning to coordinate your inner persona with your outer look, you can shop and dress with less anxiety, and avoid closet trauma.

SUMMARY

✦ Embrace the seven-step process for choosing how you want to look and dress.

✦ Keep in mind that lifestyle will affect how you dress.

✦ There are six clothing personality types.

✦ The personality type dictates how you dress and shop. You can change how you dress just by understanding your type or the type you would like to be.

✦ You can be a combination of personality types.

✦ Learn to dress from your inner vision of yourself.

CHAPTER 3

Claim Your Confidence and Be Lifted Up

*Nobody can make you feel inferior
without your consent.*

— Eleanor Roosevelt

Think of the person you have always wanted to be. How would you look? How would you act? What would you be wearing? Now imagine what it would be like if you became that person. How would you feel? What would your life be like? How would others treat you? How would you treat yourself? Now come back to the present moment but remember this new image of you. From this day forward, try to make every thought you think and action you take a step toward creating the person you want to be, both inside and out. You have defined your image and determined your clothing personality type; in part II you'll learn the Simple Principles of Conscious Dressing for outer beauty. But a crucial tool for nurturing your inner self and creating the perfect clothing look is confidence.

Owning all the right clothes and having the knowledge of how to put them together will not create the beautiful, dynamic clothing you if you haven't got confidence. With confidence as your tool you can live the dream fulfilled. You can be as beautiful as you want to be both on the inside and in your outer beauty.

To be beautiful is to be confident. Beauty comes from within and only confidence allows it to shine through and show how exceptional you really are. Marianne Williamson in her book *A Return to Love* and later Nelson Mandela in his 1994 inaugural speech said:

> We ask ourselves, who am I to be brilliant, gorgeous, talented, and fabulous?
> Actually, who are you not to be?
> You are a child of God.
> Your playing small doesn't serve the world.
> There is nothing enlightened about shrinking so that other people won't feel insecure around you.
> We were born to make manifest the glory of God that is within us.
> It's not just in some of us; it's in everyone.
> And as we let our own light shine, we unconsciously give other people permission to do the same.

What is confidence? Confidence lets you know that you are attractive even when you are not feeling your outer best. We all have moments when we do not feel our best. None of us can be perfect 24/7. When you have confidence, you know that you can be and do anything you set your mind to. It's what makes you reach for the stars and know you can get there. Confidence keeps you heading in the direction of your dreams. Confidence allows you to tap into your beauty in life. It means knowing that you are everything you need to be right now. With confidence, you know that you are sufficient and beautiful inside and out and you do not need one more of anything to make you whole and attractive.

There are four traps that keep us from being confident and connected to our beauty self:

TRAP 1. *Believing that circumstances define us*
Circumstances are not who we are. Circumstances are nothing more than moments in time. If you don't like your circumstances, take the first step by making a decision to change them. The way we look is to some extent a circumstance that we can improve on. Whether this means

changing our weight or our hair color, or simply learning to dress more flatteringly for our body type, we can make the choice to change, thereby empowering ourselves. The way we look does not define us. We are who we believe we are. Circumstances do not determine that.

TRAP 2. *Thinking that other people's opinions of us are more important than our own*

Overly focusing on what other people think of the way we look or dress means never taking responsibility for our clothing choices or personal style. We all have opinions — it's our favorite pastime. Deciding what other people should do, who they should be, or how they should look can be like a sport. Confidence is about choosing to believe in your own instincts and then standing firm in that choice. Just as clothing seasons change, so too do the opinions of others relative to the way you look. Having confidence means not focusing on what other people think and taking the time to dress based on your clothing personality and inner beauty.

TRAP 3. *Feeling that we are not enough or that we are not whole*

We may be insecure; we may feel that something is missing either in ourselves, our circumstances, or the way we look. We may feel that we are not thin enough or attractive enough, that we do not have the right look or the right clothes or the right amount of money to be happy.

Everything we need, we already have. From this knowledge we can create anything we want. When we are not confident, it is because we are looking outside ourselves for something to make us feel whole. If you don't yet feel confident, try acting as though you were, and soon enough it will become who you are.

I used to fake confidence when I was feeling insecure about myself, thinking that I somehow didn't deserve to look my best. How did I fake it? Before any situation in which I knew I had to feel confident, I would take a deep breath and then imagine myself as I wanted to be and appear. I would picture how I might look and act if I did feel confident. Using that image, I was able to step away from my insecurities and proceed forward with all the confidence I needed.

TRAP 4. *Living in pecking order comparisons*

Women who are confident believe in their own beauty without reference to others. They can look in the mirror and think, "I'm beautiful because I radiate confidence." Confident women don't wait for "if onlys"; they live their lives, make friends, and are successful because they know their beauty must come from within first.

Comparing ourselves to other people tears down our self-esteem and takes away our confidence. There will always be someone who has more than you do or is prettier than you are, and there will always be someone who has less than you do and is not as attractive as you are. Confidence is about living your own life and knowing that you have the power to change it. Comparisons take this power away from you, leaving you struggling to keep up instead of excelling.

I was in a clothing store and saw a stunning, well-dressed woman buying some clothes. She seemed happy and confident. A few minutes later as she was paying for her merchandise another woman walked into the store who was also very beautiful — but in addition she glowed with self-assurance and inner confidence. The first woman noticed the other woman and became sullen. Her mood changed almost immediately. Why? Even though this first woman had exterior beauty, it meant nothing when she compared herself to another woman who was equally as beautiful. She had in a second gone from feeling confident and attractive to feeling less than, and all for no reason. This woman did not feel beautiful inside, and this is how we must feel to have true, lasting outer beauty.

Confident women know that what other people think is possible or impossible has nothing to do with them. They set their own goals. They listen to their own opinions, which are the ones that count. They use their inner experiences or intuition as their guide and make decisions based on gut instinct. They know that their choices define them. They choose based on where they want to go and what they want to achieve. They avoid choosing based on need — need to be liked, need to feel worthy — because that is shortsighted and will limit their achievements. They are in control of who they are and where they want to go. A confident person thinks herself to confidence.

Confidence can change your life. To be confident is to know that everything will work out. Be in your confidence, and watch your world unfold.

EXERCISE
AWAKEN YOUR SELF-CONFIDENCE

Follow these ten steps to awaken your self-confidence and think your way to beauty both inside and out:

STEP 1. In your clothing journal, write down how you want to look — your ideal physical appearance. Do not include characteristics that you cannot change, such as height. Visualize who you are now and how you can improve on that vision. Include in your description how you would like to feel about who you are. (You can also include pictures cut from magazines that represent the confident image of you.)

STEP 2. Look at this description every morning when you get up and every night before you go to sleep.

STEP 3. Every day, imagine yourself as you will feel and be with the image of you fulfilled. See yourself behaving that way now. Picture this image before you go to sleep.

STEP 4. Take at least one action every day in the direction of your ideal image.

STEP 5. Look long-term but take action short-term. Keep the vision of the ideal you in your mind. Do not let circumstances determine your future. Keep your eye on the prize, and be confident that the new image of you is coming forth.

STEP 6. Look for opportunities that will take you where you want to go.

STEP 7. Put aside your ego, and be open to change.

STEP 8. Ask and ask again until you get the answer you want.

STEP 9. Don't depend on other people's opinions. Listen, but realize that the ultimate decision is yours. If you start to feel insecure, take a deep breath, picture yourself as you would like to be, then move forward.

STEP 10. Continue to stay confident, take action, and be ready, as the image of a beautiful you is becoming a reality.

By keeping these steps in mind you can go from faking confidence to being in it. These steps will allow you to focus on what's important and create a level of confidence you have never before experienced.

This is what dressing to your potential is all about — being confident. You cannot make an image mistake because the only judge is you. Judge yourself harshly and you will be frustrated by the image and clothing process. Accept and embrace yourself and you will soon be expressing your confident inner beauty self.

SUMMARY

+ To be beautiful is to be confident.

+ Learn what confidence is and how to become it.

+ There are four traps that keep us from being confident. Know what they are and how to step out of them.

+ If you don't know how to be confident, fake it until it becomes you.

+ Use the ten steps to think yourself beautiful and awaken the confidence within.

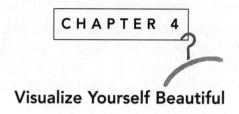

CHAPTER 4

Visualize Yourself Beautiful

*Make the most of yourself,
for that is all there is of you.*

— Ralph Waldo Emerson

Visualization is the creation of images in the mind, and it plays a key role in what we make of our lives. Every positive or negative thought that you have about yourself is eventually outwardly pictured. When you do not actively decide what picture to create of who you are, your mind still forms mental images. Many times these pictures are triggered from emotions or the way we feel about ourselves and then outwardly pictured through the way we behave and look and dress. By defining your image as described in chapter 1, you can take an active role in deciding how you want to look. Using that image, you can create a positive picture of the beautiful you in your mind through visualization. Visualize the beautiful you by simply forming a mental image of the way you want to look. Imagine how you would feel if that image became your reality, as we did with the journal exercise at the end of the last chapter.

Visualizing yourself beautiful is a simple way to see yourself in a positive light. We all have a different vision of beauty, especially relative to the clothing and dressing process. Decide what beauty is for you, then picture it in your mind either through the image previously defined or by the way you feel when you look good. Here are two ways to do this during the dressing process:

✦ *Picture yourself as you would look in an outfit wherever you plan to wear the outfit.*

When trying on clothes and deciding what to wear for any date, party, or gathering with friends or family members, always picture in your mind's eye how you want to look for that particular event. With this image in mind, if you still do not feel attractive in the clothing you're trying on, the outfit is not for you.

For example, you have been invited to a big black-tie birthday bash for a close friend. Upon receiving the invitation, panic sets in as you realize you have nothing to wear. So, you decide to buy something new. While you are out shopping and trying on evening dresses for this party, use the visualization technique described above. Try on your potential dress choices and as you look in the mirror wearing each one, try to imagine yourself with your makeup done and your hair styled as it would be the night of the party. Picture the beautiful dress matched with your accessories — chandelier earrings, sheer nylons, satin heels, rhinestone bracelet, and a beaded clutch. Then ask: "Is this dress right for me?" Your gut instinct response will tell you if it is or isn't for you. Visualizing the image of yourself as you wish to appear will help you decide on what truly will make you look and feel your best.

Another way to decide on what you want to wear is to match the image of your clothing personality type to the clothing you are trying on, then visualize your selection. For example, you have determined that you are the Actress Type so visualize yourself standing out at the party you will be attending. Which dress of the many that you are trying on will help you do that? Is it the turtleneck sweater dress? Probably not. Is it the fitted, sleeveless, short, lace and chiffon dress with a silk wrap and satin heels? Yes, that fits the Actress Type and would allow you to stand out at the party.

This process of visualizing yourself fully dressed and accessorized even before you select the outfit will help to narrow down your clothing choices and make looking good easy.

✦ *Always picture yourself beautiful no matter where you are going or what you are wearing.*

By picturing yourself looking good, you will feel better about yourself and your self-image and self-esteem will grow correspondingly. Too often we operate on remote control about the way we see ourselves; we begin an internal dialogue that is destructive instead of constructive.

What follows is a little visualization exercise you can do anywhere to change how you see yourself and silence negative thought patterns. Anytime you need a quick pick-me-up because you are either not feeling your best or do not think you look good, stop for a minute and then picture yourself beautiful. Notice how much better you feel. You can do this anywhere at any time — while shopping, trying on clothes, or just working out at the gym. For example, you are on your way to meet some friends who also happen to invite a date for you — call it a blind date. You are dressed and take that one last look in the mirror before you leave your house. Suddenly, you feel overwhelmed because the pants you are wearing make you feel big. Instead of letting anxiety kick in, take a deep breath and picture the beautiful ideal you. Now look in the mirror. In most cases you will see yourself looking better and be ready for your evening out. If you are not sure how to visualize yourself beautiful, find a picture of yourself that shows you at a moment when you looked great and happy. Study the picture and how you look, notice your expression. What is it that you feel makes you beautiful? Remember why you were so happy. Remember why you felt beautiful. Keep this memory in mind and then call it up when you need it. This positive personal image will instantly change your frame of mind. Remember the picture of the beautiful, happy you any time you find yourself in a mood trap.

There are three mood traps that can prevent us from seeing how good we look in clothes. When you find yourself in one of these traps, just step out of it by visualizing yourself beautiful.

TRAP 1. *Seeing how we feel instead of how we actually look*
We all have bad days. Off days, I call them, days when things are just off and outside influences just make us feel kind of low. If you are out shopping and feeling moody, remember to be gentle with yourself as you try on different clothes. Sometimes how you feel is not how you look. This is why one day you can put on an outfit and feel confident that you look fabulous and then the very next day, put on the same outfit and feel that you look terrible in it, as if you need to change everything about how you look.

A friend, Karen, told me about an experience she had that shows how the way other people see us is really about the attitude we project. She was up all night working on a big project for work. The next day she was exhausted and clearly didn't feel that she looked her best. She decided regardless of how she was feeling about her appearance, she would act as if she felt beautiful. She took her time and did her makeup, styled her hair, and put on a bright-colored top. Sure enough, she received many compliments that day on how great she looked even though she really didn't feel her best. It was all about attitude.

TRAP 2. *Seeing our flaws instead of our assets*
I have passed up many great clothing items because I looked at myself and saw only that wrinkle or those few extra pounds. Remember the exercise above: when you find yourself focusing too much on your flaws, change your vision by recalling yourself at your most beautiful. Our flaws are what make us interesting as human beings. If we were all perfect, there would be no need for us to grow and change. In chapter 5 you will learn that accepting your flaws is what allows you to be comfortable with who you are and dress to express that beauty.

TRAP 3. *Passing up a great clothing item because we don't know how to choose*

Defining your image and visualizing yourself beautiful will help you match the beautiful image you have of yourself with the clothes that project that image. You will become much happier, self-confident, and comfortable with choosing new clothes once you know how you want to look. You will be able to identify the right clothes for you that fit your image, your body type, and your personality.

Visualize yourself beautiful from the inside and your appearance will show it. Women who are beautiful on the inside demonstrate the following characteristics:

+ Beautiful women know how to play up their positive physical attributes. Learn what yours are, then learn how to use them to your advantage.

+ Beautiful women know that outer beauty is sustained by inner beauty. If you know this, you will always be beautiful regardless of age or weight or any other perceived flaw.

+ Beautiful women visualize themselves beautiful — they think beautiful thoughts about themselves. What are you thinking?

+ Beautiful women expect the best and keep their internal dialogue positive.

+ Beautiful women support other women. When we help other women, friends, and family members to look their best and be their best, we radiate confidence and beauty.

+ Beautiful women see themselves and the world as they want them to be and take action to make that happen. "You can't" always means "you can" and knowing this makes a woman strong and beautiful.

Our lives are shaped by how we see ourselves. It is too easy to see the negative and focus on the flaws, but much more fun to see the positive. When we are able to see the beautiful in ourselves, we are much more apt to see it in everyone else.

Here are some ways to awaken your beauty within and see how beautiful you really are. You may discover additional ways of your own to add to the list.

+ No matter what you look like when you get up in the morning, visualize yourself beautiful. Many of us go on remote control when we get up and look in the mirror, and see only flaws. Look in the mirror and say or think, "I am beautiful."

+ When getting dressed, if you see any imperfection such as a few extra pounds, turn your vision inward to see what you like about yourself. As a replacement for "I look fat" focus on something positive such as "I have great legs."

+ When you are dressed and about to leave the house, say to yourself, "I look great."

+ No matter what happens during the day, believe "you can."

+ Notice something fabulous about another woman (her hairstyle, her laugh, her smile) and then tell her.

+ When you hear any negative internal dialogue about your appearance, say "cancel, cancel" to yourself, then replace the critical thoughts with positive phrases such as "I radiate beauty."

+ Smile at everyone for no reason.

+ Choose to wear something in your closet you have never worn before and be confident in it. Notice how revitalized you feel.

+ Whenever possible throughout the day, listen to music that speaks to your inner beauty.

+ Imagine yourself in a beautiful destination, looking fabulous, then take a deep breath as if you are breathing in the experience.

SUMMARY

✦ When shopping or trying on clothes, always picture yourself as you will look with the right accessories, and with hair styled and makeup done.

✦ Picture yourself beautiful at any time for a quick self-esteem pick-me-up.

✦ Step out of the three clothing mood traps and move away from destructive internal dialogue.

✦ Use the list of ways to awaken your inner beauty and add some of your own.

✦ Know that true beauty comes from within, so always visualize yourself beautiful.

CHAPTER 5

Defy the Clothing Myths

I finally realize that I don't have to have an A-plus perfect body, and now I'm very happy with the way I am.

— Drew Barrymore

What keeps women from finding their inner beauty selves? What keeps us from looking beautiful on the outside in the clothes we choose to wear? What keeps us from knowing how beautiful we really are before we add a stitch of clothing? Only our perception of who we are stands in the way, and it must be adjusted to allow our inner self to shine forth. Looking good and knowing you look good are two different realities. Many women look good and don't know it. Accepting your flaws whatever they may be gives you the freedom to look good and know it.

We can all look consistently great in the clothes we choose to buy and wear so long as we believe we are beautiful and worthy. We all have flaws — that is the nature of the human race. When you realize that you do not have to be perfect to be interesting and unique in physical appearance and through personality, you are liberated. Once you know this, you get inspired. You can then create your own unique vision of your clothing self and implement that vision through a logical process outlined in the following three steps:

1. Make the effort to look good. Looking great is about making an effort to be in your power as a woman. That means

putting a little extra effort into the dressing process, instead of just throwing on any clothing outfit with the hope that it will make you look fabulous. Examples might include adding accessories to what you wear to make your outfits look special and unique (see chapter 8, Accessories Make an Outfit), choosing colors that complement your personal coloring (see chapter 10, Color Coordinate Your Wardrobe), highlighting your best physical features (see chapter 11, Know Your Body), and dressing to match your image and clothing personality type.

2. Know the right styles of clothing to reflect your unique beauty self. Knowing what clothing looks good on you comes from knowing your body and learning to highlight your most positive physical attributes.

3. Learn to control your emotional state. Women who have control over their emotional state when it comes to getting dressed are in their power as women. They understand what looks good on them and they know how to show off their inner beauty in the way they present themselves. When we cannot see how good we look in clothing, it may be because we are dressing from an emotional need to fit in or stand out, rather than to express who we are.

Our inner self is our guide in creating the vision of who we are. This vision directs what we choose to focus on, and what we choose to focus on affects the way we feel about ourselves and interact with clothing.

If we focus on our negative emotions — not feeling enough (thin enough, wealthy enough, pretty enough), not feeling worthy (I don't deserve to look good), or feeling fearful (afraid of what people will think, fear of not being accepted) — then we lose sight of how beautiful we really are. If we stay in our positive emotions — confidence (I am great no matter what), awareness (I know who I am), and an entitled sense of worth (I'm worth it) — then we feel good about the way we look and the way we dress. Remember: the most basic aspect of looking good is feeling good. Focusing your attention on the positive aspects of your beauty will make you feel good.

Consequently, you are able to focus on things that are great about who you are and how you look. Whatever you focus on EXPANDS. So, focus on something great about you.

Some women look beautiful no matter what they are wearing. They know how to choose clothes and they look beautifully dressed all the time. How are these women different from other women? They are just like all of us — except that they focus less on their negative emotions and instead turn their energy toward being beautiful by highlighting their positive body attributes and showing the world their charismatic selves. They focus on maximizing their positive emotions — such as confidence.

Below are the characteristics of a woman who focuses on how beautiful she really is and in turn is able to dress to look great:

✦ She sees her flaws as part of her whole self. When her flaws are taken together with her strengths, everything about her is part of her unique beauty.

✦ She knows that whatever extra weight she may have does not determine her worth. She may lose or gain weight but that does not change her value in the world.

✦ She knows that physical beauty is only skin deep and fleeting, but inner beauty is forever.

✦ She understands her positive physical attributes and knows how to play them up.

✦ She dresses to please herself because she knows other people's opinions can be fickle.

✦ She is confident and carries this confidence with her regardless of what she is wearing.

A woman who knows instinctively how to dress well, knows the effect she creates has nothing to do with being thin or drop-dead gorgeous. She is able to choose clothing that is right for her because what she selects reflects who she is — her inner beauty. She accepts her flaws and this makes her beautiful from the inside out.

There are many obstacles to achieving this feeling of confidence in the way we dress. Among these obstacles are myths that most of us have probably at one time or another taken as facts, sabotaging our self-confidence and focusing our attention on negative emotions. Here are five myths that may keep you from creating an image that reflects your true inner beauty through fashion:

MYTH 1. *To look good and be confident you must be thin.* Not true. As described above, there are plenty of women who never feel really attractive no matter how thin they are. There are also many beautiful women who have style and a few extra pounds.

Looking your best is not about weight. It is about creating a personal image that reflects who you are. It's about reflecting on the outside the person you really are on the inside. You look great when you are in your power as a woman and accepting and flaunting that power. When I was younger, I had a boyfriend who was obsessed with my weight. I was a size four and he thought I should starve myself into a smaller size. Being younger than him and insecure, I assumed he knew what he was talking about. When I finally broke up with him I stepped into my power as a woman and learned that what he thought was irrelevant. Only I can determine my worth, and the size of my waist cannot set my personal value.

Susan has blonde hair, big green eyes, and a dynamic personality — and she knows all about stepping into her power as a woman. She is confident and charismatic and has a great career and a loving husband. She is in her power as a woman and feels good about herself, no matter what, and she radiates beauty. She also happens to be a size fourteen. She would like to lose some weight, but that process is not going to stop her from being the best she can be today. She can shop and select exactly the right clothes for her body type better than most women I know.

If you feel you are overweight, don't put off dressing to reflect who you are until you get to your optimal size, and don't let someone else determine the vision of who you are. Too often we sacrifice who we are now and focus on some end-of-the-rainbow later date. In reality, we only have each moment to be who we are. There is probably no one better known for this philosophy than talk show host Oprah Winfrey. If the myth about weight were really true, it would belie the astronomical success she has had and contradict everything the world knows about one of its most popular citizens!

I know many beautiful women who are radiant and charismatic but not thin. I also know women who are thin but are not comfortable with who they are. Weight is a big issue for most women in our society. It has become an obsession, but we don't have to buy into that obsession. Looking good is about feeling confident regardless of weight or any other external issues. Coming from a place of confidence, we let others know that they can either take us or leave us — this is who we are, and we are proud of it.

MYTH 2. *You have to be a creative genius to know how to dress well.*
Not true. You just have to know what works for you — for your body type and personality and for the image you want to create. If you narrow the focus from what looks good on others to what looks good on you, you can become expert in dressing to express yourself. If you focus on dressing yourself and stop comparing yourself to others, you will be much happier, and dressing will become much easier. You don't have to be born a creative genius to look good.

Fashion is creative — there is no doubt about that — but the process of assembling a good wardrobe is also logical. By shifting your thought process you can learn what really looks good on you and what enhances the image you want to create and project into the world.

MYTH 3. *I am not pretty enough to look fashionable, so it doesn't really matter what I wear.*
Not true. If you are habitually comparing yourself to supermodels in fashion magazines, you may well feel like you're not pretty enough. Who in the world can compare herself favorably with the seemingly flawless women in high-fashion advertisements?

Each of us has some physical qualities that are attractive to other people — for example, lovely eyes, a warm smile, shiny hair, high cheekbones, a prominent bustline, or slender hips — we just need to figure out what these attributes are and then play them up appropriately. I know a woman who is overweight and also big-busted. She always wears V-neck style suit shirts, open just wide enough to show off her cleavage, thereby deflecting the focus away from her extra weight. These tops are attractive and classy-looking and also allow her to play up her more attractive attributes. When you know how to dress to reflect your own uniqueness, you are creating a calling card for the world.

MYTH 4. *If I look too good, I will make other women uncomfortable and resentful, and they won't like me.*
Buying into this myth results in playing yourself down — not being the best you can be because you are afraid of what others will think. Playing yourself down sabotages your ability to express who you are and feel really good about it. It's difficult to think about what looks best on you when you're busy worrying about the opinions and emotions of others. When you radiate confidence and self-esteem, coupled with genuine concern for others (see the characteristics of a woman with inner beauty in the Introduction), you'll be met with a positive reaction, not resentment. When you finally allow the real you to come to the surface, you can make positive changes in the way you look by daring to reflect your maximum potential with what you wear.

Dressing to look your best and aiming for your full potential becomes possible once you accept how great you really are. People will like and respect you for expressing who you are. If someone else isn't happy because you look too good for their comfort, realize that it is not about you at all — it's about their insecurities. Look your best, and enjoy it.

MYTH 5. *I have to spend a lot of money on clothes to look good.*
No, you don't. The Simple Principles for Conscious Dressing you will learn about in part II show you how to assemble a

wardrobe logically, so that you may purchase key pieces of clothing and accessory items that you can keep and wear virtually forever. By limiting mistaken purchases, you can minimize the amount of money you spend on clothing and still look great all the time. Looking good is not about wearing the most expensive or most trendy clothes you can find. It is about wearing clothes that make you look and feel your best. If your budget is limited, you can find great pieces on sale or even discover treasures at discount stores, resale boutiques, or secondhand clothing shops.

Falling for any of these clothing myths may keep you from living up to your potential in the way you dress. Now is the time to be the best you can be through beauty and image. You can do this by stepping into your power as a woman and accepting your true worth.

SUMMARY

+ Our beauty self creates the vision of who we are. Our vision determines what we focus on.

+ We can implement the vision of our clothing self by making the extra effort to look good, learning to dress for our specific body type, and gaining control over our emotional states.

+ Using the three simple steps for focusing your attention on positive emotions can make you feel beautiful all day.

+ What we focus on E X P A N D S.

+ Understanding the six characteristics of a beautiful woman enables you to become one inside and out.

+ The five clothing myths can keep you from creating the image you want and dressing to your potential — don't believe them.

CHAPTER 6

Tame Your Clothing Emotions

*I think women see me on the cover of magazines
and think I never have a pimple or bags under my eyes.
You have to realize that's after two hours of hair
and makeup, plus retouching. Even I don't wake
up looking like Cindy Crawford.*

— Cindy Crawford

Clothing is a means of expression. Clothes are the tools the wearer uses to create an image. Just as paint and paintbrushes are the tools a painter uses to express her artistic vision, so too is clothing used to reflect our visions of ourselves. How do we know what to wear to reflect this vision? How do we discover and shape our own vision? If dressing is like art, and we are allowed free expression, then why don't we feel free to express ourselves through clothing? Our emotions control our vision of who we are and many times they may override our ability to think logically. This is why understanding of and control over your emotional state are the keys to creating the vision of your perfect clothing self. By understanding your emotions and why they are triggered during the dressing process, you gain greater control in crafting the picture of who you want to be and how you want to look, without emotional static. Then you can implement that vision using the Simple Principles for Conscious Dressing in part II.

Why do our emotions hold us back from dressing to express this vision of ourselves? Where do these emotions related to clothing come from? How and why are these emotions triggered? To figure out the answers to all of these questions, we need to explore our earliest memories of clothing and self-image. How we feel about ourselves in clothes and what we choose to buy and wear as adults are directly linked to our childhood clothing experiences and the images we may have developed of ourselves.

Think back in time. What are your first clothing memories? Do you remember what you liked to wear as a child? At what age did you become aware of clothing and how clothing made you look and feel? Are there types of clothing that you won't wear today because of negative childhood clothing experiences?

I met a woman recently who rarely wears skirts because growing up she was forced to wear them every day as part of a school uniform. She hadn't realized why she had such an aversion to skirts until we explored her childhood clothing experiences. She was overweight and the required school uniform included a gray skirt that fell just at the knee level. Her skirt always rose up slightly because of her extra weight around the stomach area, causing her thighs to show. This made her even more self-conscious. Today, she is thin by societal standards but still feels overweight when wearing a skirt because of this childhood experience.

Were you one of those girls who got all dressed up in your mother's clothes, or were you the tomboy wanting nothing to do with "cute" girl clothes? Did you have weight issues as a child — either the clothes you wore were too small or too big? Did you wear clothing hand-me-downs or did you have a lot of new clothes every year? Did your family have money to spend on clothes or not at all? As a child, were you aware that what you wore or how you presented yourself affected the way others treated you?

Mary was always the best-dressed girl in her school. She even received a school award from her classmates for best dressed. Needless to say she was very popular and wanted to stay that way. This meant that every day without fail, Mary had to get dressed to look her best. Then there is Kate, who when she was in school was self-conscious and never knew what to wear. She did not fit in but never really stood out. Her experiences are very different from Mary's.

Depending on our childhood experiences with clothing, many of us end up having a very strange relationship with clothes as adults. We (1) don't know what to wear, (2) copy what we saw growing up, or (3) feel strongly about what we want to wear. Without even being aware of it, many of us have fallen into an emotional clothing pattern that still guides how we shop and dress today.

This pattern relative to the clothing process is driven by unresolved self-esteem issues from childhood. These clothing and image emotions affect how we see ourselves, and they hold us back from really expressing who we are. They affect the way we dress, shop, and interact with clothing. For many of us, negative and sometimes positive emotions regarding our image or anything clothing related can seem to show up out of nowhere; but they actually do come from somewhere specific. When a childhood memory relative to image is triggered, our self-esteem is affected and we feel the clothing and image emotions from that experience. As crazy as it may seem, image and clothing experiences often create the "dressing crazies" for many of us as adults — whether it be that out-of-control feeling we get when we just do not know what to wear to look good or the constant need to shop and buy clothing to maintain a certain image. The good news is that by uncovering and understanding these past issues, we can change the way we see ourselves, and thus our self-image.

In order to define our emotional issues around the dressing process, I have identified four emotional patterns that drive our image and clothing experiences. Each pattern describes the emotional triggers that dictate how we feel about ourselves and behave when buying clothes or getting dressed. One pattern may ring true for you, or your image and clothing emotions may be expressed by a combination of the patterns described below.

Identifying your emotional pattern or patterns will allow you to understand why the process of clothes shopping and getting dressed affects you the way it does. Stripping away and setting aside clothing and image emotions enables you to view the process of shopping and dressing logically. By becoming aware of why you choose the clothing you do and what triggers your emotions, you can stop clothing anxiety before it starts. Once you are in control of your emotions, you can create a more comfortable, confident, and beautifully dressed you.

The four emotional patterns that influence the way we shop, the clothing we buy, and the way we dress are:

+ *The Overachiever:* This is the emotional pattern of a person who feels she always has to look and be perfect. The emotion is "I need to be perfect and look that way" or "I need to show how special I am."

+ *The Accumulator:* This is the emotional pattern of a person who feels the need to accumulate as many clothes (and often other possessions) as possible. The emotion is "I do not know who I am" or "I am not feeling whole."

+ *The Moderate:* This is the emotional pattern of a person who does everything in moderation, even the way she dresses. The emotion is "I need to fit in" or "I don't want to make other people feel uncomfortable."

+ *The Depriver:* This is the emotional pattern of a person who has a minimal interest in clothing or image, or deprives herself of the right to look and feel good. The emotion is "I do not feel deserving" or "I feel guilty."

Let's look at each pattern in detail.

THE OVERACHIEVER

The Overachievers' pattern is an obsession with perfection, be it in the way they look or the things they do. Overachievers care a great deal about what people think of them; they want to be respected. If they don't look their best at all times, they don't feel their best. They hide feelings of insecurity, and may have grown up looking or feeling different from other people either through economic status, ethnicity, nationality, or color. They may have also had strong discipline to be the perfect child or felt the need to stand out among numerous siblings or excel in any area to get away from their environment. Their self-esteem is directly tied to looking like a million dollars.

The Overachiever's Story

Talia fits the pattern of an Overachiever perfectly. She grew up in the inner city raised by a single mother. Her family was economically challenged and did not have extra money to spend on clothes, so she always wore hand-me-down clothes that came from family friends or charitable organizations. She worked hard all through school to get good grades. She knew at a young age that in order for her to have a better life she had to go to college, which meant getting a scholarship. She got a job with a Fortune 500 company out of college and worked her way up into a senior level position. Every week the division she manages has a meeting to discuss business matters. Talia feels that she has to be dressed impeccably in the most expensive, perfectly fitted and tailored clothes, in order for her to be accepted by her employees. She shops for a new outfit every week so she can dazzle them with her perfect persona. She spends a good portion of her income on clothing but would prefer to see some of that money go into funding a retirement account. Talia needs to accept that she has achieved her place in the company because she has earned it, not just because she looks perfect. She is judging herself as the child she was, trying to distance herself from the child who wore the hand-me-down clothing, and to do so she feels she has to wear the best that money can buy at all times.

To overcome these feelings, Talia should remind herself that she is truly a successful woman by reviewing her accomplishments — college and a high-level corporate position, all from modest beginnings. This will help her see that she is no longer that little girl in hand-me-down clothing. She should acknowledge her need to dress well and learn to dress well without spending everything she earns on her wardrobe. Her childhood clothing experiences have affected her self-esteem and still dictate how she behaves and dresses today.

Talia starts slow by first recognizing her difficult childhood. When she shops and dresses for her business meetings, this child inside keeps telling her that she needs to be perfect. Talia lets this child inside know how much she respects her strength but that she is a woman now and can look great without being obsessive about it. Instead of buying a new outfit every week for her meeting, Talia begins to mix and match the high-end clothing she already owns. One week she wears her Armani suit with a crisp white shirt. The next week she wears the Armani suit pants with a black turtleneck and a Hermès scarf. This is a huge leap for Talia, but she steps into her confidence in week two to carry it off. She realizes that she can still look great and be respected for who she is and her abilities without having to buy new clothes every week.

Talia is a combination of the Socialite and the Classic personality types. She spends a lot of her time, prior to work or going out, grooming to get her makeup and hair perfect. She likes designer wardrobe items but also likes to be classic when the event calls for it. She makes up for any insecurity she may have in this new way of thinking with confidence and an entitled sense of worth.

The Overachiever Wardrobe Tips

The key to transcending the Overachiever pattern and gaining control of your emotional state is to remind yourself that you have earned the life you are experiencing as a woman today. Acknowledge who you were in childhood; bless that girl (you) for being so strong. Accept your need to dress well and be okay with it. The little girl that was you made the successful woman that you have become. From this point of awareness you can then begin to assemble a wardrobe that makes looking perfect easy without costing everything you make. Once you overcome this Overachiever pattern, you will be able to look fabulous and perfect without having to buy a new outfit every day or every week as in Talia's case. You will be able to limit your negative emotions relative to clothing and image because you have acknowledged where this need to be perfect is coming from. When you feel anxiety while shopping or getting dressed, connect with the little girl inside you by letting her know it is okay to feel the way she does. Let her (you) know that you are a grown-up, beautiful woman now who is dressing to express herself today. Since Talia has defined who she is and how she wants to look, all she needs now is to learn simple ways to express that in the clothing she chooses to wear and buy.

If you fall into this Overachiever pattern, here are some ways to make assembling a wardrobe and the perfect clothing image easy. Using these tools will allow you to view the clothing process logically and step away from the emotional pattern that has kept you in a place of fear for so long.

- Focus on buying key quality clothing items for your wardrobe such as high-end coats and leather pieces that will stay in fashion and can be worn for many years. Aiming for high-end quality will eliminate the need to buy in quantity, and will allow you to put together perfect outfits easily.

- Suits are versatile and can be worn for many different occasions. Adding suits to your wardrobe makes getting dressed easy and somewhat stress free. Suits can be worn almost anywhere: work, a black-tie party, lunch with friends. Pairing a suit with a camisole can create a fun, flirty look; a turtleneck can give it a more sophisticated look.

- Spend money on accessory items; they will increase the value and look of your wardrobe tenfold. (See chapter 8.) Choose accessories that are in line with your clothing personality to create the perfect "put-together" look.

- Buy a few key pieces such as black pants that go with everything, then you can afford to spend more money on different tops or designer jackets to go with the black pants. This creates a simple but perfect look.

- See chapter 9, Good Quality Never Goes Out of Style, to find out how to select quality clothing items.

THE ACCUMULATOR

Accumulators buy clothes and other possessions all the time regardless of what they already own or what they need. They thrive on the excitement of the purchase; a new item means a new them. It means they have the power to say, "I can buy what I want," and are in control, even though they may never wear all the clothes they purchase. They are into accumulating clothes because they have either never defined who they are or they need to make themselves feel worthy. They think if they buy more, they will have more to wear, but they still end up wearing the same clothes over and over again. Accumulators typically had strong childhood influences from a parent or sibling and because of this, they never truly developed a sense of self; this is why they keep accumulating more and more. Without this strong sense of self, their worth becomes tied to what they own and buy. Some Accumulators grew up with the anxiety associated with family separation or divorce, which has created a void and a need in their adult lives to fill up or feel worthy.

The Accumulator's Story

Jenny fits the Accumulator pattern. She grew up with a mother who was very domineering. Jenny's father lived and worked in a different state and although her parents never got divorced, they were not together all the time. Jenny got married very young to a man who also had strong opinions and was somewhat controlling. As a child Jenny wore clothes that her mother picked out and then as an adult, she got a lot of input from her husband about what looked good on her. Because of these strong influences, Jenny never developed a strong sense of self. She never defined herself as a person because those around her did that for her and as such she never developed a feeling of worth.

Jenny needs to begin to define who she is. She can do this by first making a freestyle list of her likes and dislikes. She can then select words that describe her values. What is important to her? What does she value about who she is? Does she value honesty or freedom or commitment most? These two steps will begin to give Jenny a sense of who she is as a person. By creating a picture of who she is inside, Jenny can then decide how she wants to look on the outside through image and clothing.

Jenny begins to get a sense of who she is and starts to form her own definition of herself. With this definition, she then defines her image. She has an Actress Type personality but has been living as the Sporty Type for too long to fit her mother's and spouse's definitions of who they wanted her to be. No wonder she is overwhelmed and not sure what to buy and wear. Jenny uses the Seven Secrets for Expressing the Inner You to help her determine who she is and who she wants to be. Now she is finally finding herself, and these days when she shops she looks for clothing items that fit her image, personality, and body type.

The Accumulator Wardrobe Tips

The key to transcending the Accumulator pattern and gaining control of your emotions is to establish a clear vision of who you are. To do this, get a sense of your likes, dislikes, and values. Only when you define who you are can you know how you want to look. Once you have a clearer sense of self and worth, shopping will no longer be about filling up on purchases. You will have a much better idea what you are looking for — and why. Take inventory of what you own and then simplify (chapters 15 and 16). This step is essential for Accumulators, because they may have more than what they need or they may find they have plenty of the wrong clothing styles for who they are now. Simplifying the dressing process through an organized approach and matching our real self-image and vision with what we wear eliminates closet trauma. If you fall into this pattern, here are some ways to make crafting a clear clothing vision of you easy.

+ Define your image: know how you want to look so you may more appropriately buy what fits your personality type.

+ Take the first step in simplifying your life by cleaning out your closet and making space so that you may see clearly. (See chapter 14, Getting Organized Means Finding Clothing Bliss.)

+ If you are not comfortable getting rid of clothes just yet, put them in storage, then simplify.

+ Go through each clothing item in your closet. If you would not buy the item today, get rid of it unless it is a quality clothing item.

+ Learn how to keep it clothing simple.

THE MODERATE

The Moderates' pattern is one of moderation. They will buy clothes depending on their need at the time. They may buy high-end items or everyday items. They spend more on clothes than they think because they buy items on impulse. This behavior usually signals that they are not sure what looks good on them or they don't keep track of what they own or how much they spend. They do not believe that clothes define them, yet sometimes they want to wear clothes that set them apart or make them stand out at a party or special event. Moderates act as if they do not really care about fashion, but they readily seek advice on how to dress better from anyone who seems to know how. Their self-esteem is not directly affected by how they look on a day-to-day basis, but they are concerned about how they look and fit in at a social level. They dress their best when going to see others, signaling that they do care what other people think. While growing up they may have had strong influences that affected their ability to make decisions relative to image. Because of this they dress to make others comfortable or so as not to rock the boat.

The Moderate's Story

Lindsey is a perfect example of a moderate. She will make a limited effort to look good if she is just running around and doesn't expect to see anyone who knows her. She cares a great deal about what she wears when seeing friends or family even for a casual lunch. She grew up with her stepsister telling her how she should look and dress and always letting her know when she didn't look her best. This sibling's opinions were very strong and had an impact on Lindsay's self-esteem and the way she dresses. Lindsey's stepsister was older than her and always had to look better than Lindsey. As a child if Lindsey looked too cute in the clothes she wore, her stepsister would tell her that she looked terrible and suggest that she change. This caused Lindsey to always wear clothing that played down her physical assets. She wanted the approval of her older stepsister and because of this never developed an image of her own. Unlike the Accumulator, the Moderate does have a strong sense of self in other areas of her life, but has made image less important because she doesn't know how she wants to look. She has either played herself down for too long or not dressed to her potential so that other people will feel comfortable around her. She worries sometimes that if she looks too good people won't like her. It is a feeling that comes directly from her childhood clothing experiences.

Lindsey needs to decide how she wants to look relative to her personality and comfort level. Reviewing the personality types will give her an idea of how she wants to dress to match who she is inside. In examining the personality types, Lindsey realizes she is actually the Artist Type. She loves free-flowing clothing that does not cling to her body but whose designs, fabric, and color show off her creativity and personality. Now that she has selected her personality type, Lindsey's bigger issue is learning to stop playing herself down. She needs to accept herself and take a stand for her own style. Confidence will help her dress for who she really is and live in that potential. With confidence, she can then define her image and begin to understand what fits her body type. She can then dress to express exactly the person she has defined herself to be.

The Moderate Wardrobe Tips

The key to transcending the Moderate pattern and gaining control of your emotional state is to develop a clear vision of how you want to look relative to clothing and image. Learn that the way you look does not determine whether someone will like or approve of you. That comes from within. Start slowly by wearing something that shows off the real you and lead with confidence. Realize that you are no longer that little girl looking for approval. Notice how people treat you when you dress to express and act with confidence. Simplify the purchasing process by only buying items that fit with that clear vision of the real clothing you:

✦ Define your perfect image and select your clothing personality using the methods detailed in chapters 1 and 2.

✦ Identify key wardrobe clothing items that you can wear for everyday use — for instance, a pair of designer jeans that will look good with any top.

✦ If you wear suits to work, buy traditional colors such as blue and black and then dress them up or down with great-looking tops.

✦ Begin to understand the types and styles of clothes that
look best on you so that you can pick clothes more easily.
(See chapter 11, Know Your Body.)

THE DEPRIVER

Deprivers either don't know what looks good on them or feel that
they don't look good in whatever they wear. They are self-critical,
and may have a lot of past emotions with which they have never
dealt. They are less accepting of their own flaws, physical or otherwise, than those people close to them. They may have issues with
forgiveness; specifically, they may have not forgiven themselves for
past misdeeds. They will wear the same clothes over and over again
without caring about the way they look. They figure, why bother,
what's the point? Deprivers will spend money on other items so
long as they are not related to image. They may have grown up in
a difficult family environment where most messages were negative.
They may have guilt related to something they did in the past that
they never came to terms with. Deprivers can look great in clothes
if they make the effort to do so.

The Depriver's Story

Karen fits the Depriver type. She carries around a lot of anger and
unfinished business from years past and is very self-conscious.
She uses clothes to hide herself, always wearing the same out-fits,
usually in dark colors, over and over again, even when they are
threadbare. In all the years I have known her, I have never seen her in
anything else. She feels guilt because she is estranged from her family and has been so for many years. When she first got married, her
parents did not approve of her husband and forced her to choose
between them and him. To this day she feels guilt about not being
able to mend that relationship. She has a great personality and is a
lot of fun but also denies herself the right to express her beauty
through image. If she made a small effort and a small investment in
her wardrobe she could look great and in turn possibly feel better
about her outer image. Karen needs to begin to understand her feelings and specifically the guilt she carries around from the past. She

needs to start by forgiving herself. She may want to make a list of all the things she forgives herself for and then all the things that make her a great human being. She needs to take responsibility for her choices and realize she can take action today to try and mend those broken relationships, if it's at all feasible. If it doesn't work out, at least she will have made the effort. When she starts to see herself with more clarity, she can begin to work on her outer image. When she looks good, it will help her to feel better about who she is.

To help her see how she would like to look and begin to focus her mind on how truly worthy she is, Karen should use visualization. Visualizing herself beautiful is a step that can be done anywhere at any time when she is feeling self-conscious or bad about who she is. With visualization she can begin to get a sense of how she wants to look. With confidence and visualization, as well as by working on forgiveness, Karen can begin to define her image by choosing her five magic image words.

The Depriver Wardrobe Tips

The key to transcending the Depriver pattern and freeing yourself from negative experiences of the past is to form a better mental picture of who you are and then forgive yourself and others. Learn that the only way to move forward in life is to release the past and deal with any issues related to it, as it can't be relived or changed. Realize you are not alone; we all have issues from the past that we must deal with. Nobody is perfect but that is what makes us special. Change can come only when you are able to forgive yourself. Only then can you see clearly who you are now. You can make better choices going forward because you were able to learn and grow from the past. With this better mental picture, you may begin to dress the part of a woman who knows her own worth. Here are some ways to help you do that:

✦ Work on your self-confidence.

✦ Use visualization to form a better picture of who you are both inside and out and learn to see yourself as already enough.

✦ Work on the image you would like to create using magic image words from chapter 1 and choose your clothing personality.

✦ Work on your mental picture and then start small by buying one new item to add to your wardrobe, maybe a new top to fit with your newly defined image and body type.

Many of us may see ourselves in more than one of these emotional patterns. At different points in your life you may experience the pattern of a Moderate and then as certain emotions are triggered, such as not feeling enough, you may binge shop and your pattern may change to that of an Accumulator.

Think about your story. We all carry around these hidden dramas from our past that play themselves out when we go shopping for clothes or have to get dressed. By identifying your emotional clothing pattern you can begin to understand the causes of closet trauma. By defining your ideal beauty self and learning how to dress using the Simple Principles for Conscious Dressing, you can release and heal these clothing and image emotions once and for all.

SUMMARY

✦ Childhood clothing experiences affect the way we dress today.

✦ Clothing and image emotions are triggered by unresolved self-esteem issues.

✦ There are four emotional patterns that affect our clothing selection and dressing process.

✦ By understanding our clothing and image emotions we can heal closet trauma.

CHAPTER 7

Control Your Communication Style by Connecting Your Inner and Outer Beauty

I don't design clothes. I design dreams.

— Ralph Lauren

We all experience some form of internal dialogue. During the day, when our attention isn't directly engaged with something or someone else, there's a constant monologue going on in our heads, mostly useful — noting our surroundings, thinking ahead to things we must remember to do, recalling events at work the previous day. But when we turn to trying on new clothes or choosing an outfit from our closet, that inner voice takes over and provides unlimited dialogue about the way we look. Sometimes the dialogue is positive, but when we experience closet trauma it is mostly negative.

Having tamed our clothing emotions, we need to take the next step toward healing closet trauma by learning to change the way we communicate with ourselves when getting dressed — what I call our communication style. As we saw in the last chapter, taming our emotions helps us to become more aware of our self-image and the clothing process. We can expand that awareness to control the internal dialogue that seeks to exploit our negative emotions about how we look and dress. Our internal dialogue — that constant inner commentary — dictates the level of anxiety and closet trauma we may feel, but it can also tell us when to feel great about the way we look or dress.

Many of us are not even aware that we are communicating with ourselves when getting dressed or shopping. When emotions are triggered relative to the clothing and image process, our internal dialogue takes over. The following steps show how our communication style affects the way we feel during the dressing process, in this case, dressing for a dinner party with friends.

STEP 1. You are aware that it is time to get dressed.

STEP 2. You open the closet and ask yourself: "What should I wear?" This question triggers all sorts of feelings and emotions.

STEP 3. Emotions are triggered. What emotional pattern takes over? Are you the Overachiever, compelled to look perfect? Are you an Accumulator, surrounded by so many clothes it seems impossible to choose what to wear? Are you a Moderate, in need of outside opinions to dress yourself? Are you a Depriver, inclined to wear the same sort of thing you always do? Your clothing emotions may not kick in until the searching phase (step 4), or they may arise just by anticipating it.

STEP 4. You search for the "right" clothes to wear. Depending on the intensity of your emotions at this point, you may be tossing clothes aside as you try on and reject various clothing choices. If you have selected your clothing personality type, by now you will have a clearer picture of how you want to look and the dressing process should become easier.

STEP 5. You engage in an internal communication process. This process may occur simultaneously during steps 3 and 4, depending on the level of your clothing anxiety. The internal process may be either positive, negative, or a combination of both. If it is negative, it may sound something like "I don't have anything to wear," "Nothing fits me right," "Why can't I lose weight?" If it is positive, it may sound something like "This top looks great on me," "I love this outfit," "I look fit." You may also have a combination of both the negative and positive dialogue.

STEP 6. You select clothes. This may be a simple process or a very complex and difficult one. As stated in step 4, if you have selected your clothing personality type to match who you are on the inside, this step is easier to move through.
STEP 7. You (finally) get dressed.
STEP 8. You check yourself out in the mirror one more time before leaving. You may then feel anxiety after the fact and feel driven to change clothes several more times before you finally leave for dinner.

EXERCISE
LISTENING TO YOUR INNER DIALOGUE

The next time you are getting dressed, when you enter steps 3 to 5 above, listen to yourself. What is your internal dialogue? What do you think or say to yourself during the dressing process? Is your internal dialogue negative: "I look terrible," "Nothing fits me right"? Is your internal dialogue positive: "I look great," "Everything fits me well"? Is your internal dialogue a mix of positive and negative?

My friend Kim shared with me some of her experiences with closet trauma. She told me that she will sometimes leave the house, get in her car, and drive away only to turn around and come back to change into something else that would make her feel more attractive. Her internal dialogue is mostly negative as her emotions are triggered during steps 3 to 5 of the dressing process: "Nothing fits me right. Why can't I find anything to wear? I need to go shopping. I don't want to go out tonight. What will everyone else be wearing?" This dialogue continues even after she is dressed and on her way to her destination.

This type of internal dialogue is triggered when we experience closet trauma, which occurs for one of the following three reasons:

✦ A lack of understanding of the emotions that keep us from looking and feeling our best — *our emotional clothing pattern.*

✦ Not having defined how we want to look — *our clothing personality and image.*

✦ Not having learned how to select the right clothing to reflect our unique positive physical attributes — *our body type.*

By understanding our clothing emotions, defining our image, and knowing our body type, we can begin to heal closet trauma and our communication style can grow to be more positive.

A woman's communication style is influenced by how connected she is to her own beauty self, that is, her ability to reflect her inner beauty through her outer beauty in the way she dresses. There are three communication styles:

STYLE 1. *Very Connected* — *Positive Communication Style*
If a woman has identified and connected to her inner beauty and implemented the Simple Principles for Conscious Dressing, she will be very connected in her communication style and her internal dialogue will be mostly positive. She knows who she is and she accepts herself fully, even her flaws. She knows how to dress her body type and keeps her closet organized so the dressing process is easy. She says to herself, "I know exactly what to wear." After a little thought, she selects her clothing and gets dressed, with minimal anxiety. Once dressed, she looks in the mirror and thinks, "This looks good." It's that simple for her.

STYLE 2. *Moderately Connected* — *Positive and Negative Communication Style*
This woman has an idea of how to dress but still experiences closet trauma some of the time. She is better connected to her inner self, but still requires some form of external validation. She knows just enough about what to wear, but has not added her own creative flair. She worries about whether she will be dressed appropriately and fit in and whether others will like what she is wearing. Her

internal dialogue is mostly positive, but she may also suc-
cumb to negative internal dialogue at times, expressing her
self-doubt with thoughts like "I have nothing to wear," or
"I'm so fat (or thin)," or "These pants make my hips look
huge," or "Why do I have to go to this dinner tonight?"
or "I feel pressured," or "Why can't this just be easy?" or
"I hate this anxiety." When she does find the right outfit
to make her look and feel good, her dialogue becomes positive: "This outfit makes my legs look thin."

No matter how early she starts the dressing process,
she often finds herself pressed for time. She may fre-
quently end up with an angry boyfriend or spouse telling
her to hurry up, or she may show up late. This woman has
typically not defined her body type or determined pre-
cisely what looks good on her. Consequently, she ends up
with too many clothing choices and doesn't know exactly
what to wear to look good consistently. Most women fall
into this communication style.

STYLE 3. *Limited Connection* — *Negative Communication
Style*
The final communication style is related to a woman with
a very limited understanding of the way she wants to look.
She may not have defined her clothing self or come to
understand the value of expressing her inner beauty
through her outer appearance. She doesn't know much
about how to dress, though she would like to learn about
the clothing process and is open and willing to listen. Her
internal dialogue is more likely to be negative, not very
supportive or confident (style 1) but not frantic either
(style 2). She may say to herself: "I don't really care how I
look," or "I'd just as soon be comfortable," or "I'll just
wear what I always wear." She gets dressed without much
careful thought about what to wear or why. She has not
defined her body type.

Most of us enter step 3 of the dressing process (emotions triggered),
and immediately go on automatic pilot, but the woman experiencing

communication style 1 doesn't because she is filled with confidence and healthy self-esteem. She knows what to wear to maximize her beauty potential and does so regardless of other people's opinions. She remains present and in control of the dressing process, selecting what to wear logically based on where she's going, the image she wishes to create, and her particular body type.

To get to communication style 1 — to be very connected to your inner beauty — you have to learn how to dress for your own unique individual body type and image, and that is what the Simple Principles for Conscious Dressing, starting with the following chapter, will show how to do.

When we dress on automatic pilot, we lose our ability to view the dressing process logically and focus on the moment at hand. In this reactive state, we bring every emotion related to self-esteem into the dressing experience.

Taking control of your internal communication and learning how to dress to reflect your inner beauty will help to limit clothing anxiety and closet trauma. Here are some methods you can use to take control of your communication style:

✦ Don't allow yourself to go on automatic pilot. Be fully present and aware.

✦ Change your communication style. When you notice yourself slipping into negative inner dialogue, immediately validate the way you look by changing that dialogue to something positive: "This blue silk blouse brings out the color of my eyes!" or "This pink pencil skirt makes my legs look sexy." You can even say a positive phrase out loud. This method will bring you into the present moment.

✦ Change your focus. You can change the way you see yourself and what you focus on. You put on a pair of white pants with a blue and white striped top and you think it looks good, but you are not sure if the pants fit right or the top makes you look wide across the bustline. Instead of seeing the flaws in the outfit or your body, notice what you like about the way it makes you look. The top makes your waist look tiny and the pants flatter your legs and once you put on accessories to complete the outfit — silver hoop earrings and white sandals with a Christian Dior jean tote — the outfit looks great for a day with friends. Always focus on something good about yourself, even if it is only that the color of your blouse makes your eyes stand out.

By changing the way you communicate with yourself, you can banish closet trauma and make clothing decisions that play up your own best attributes. Then, dressing becomes easy — even fun.

SUMMARY

✦ Communication style controls our internal dialogue when we are getting dressed.

✦ Negative internal dialogue is triggered when we experience closet trauma.

✦ There are three communication styles that affect the way you relate to yourself during the dressing process.

✦ Taking control of your communication style is done by defining your image, knowing your body type, understanding your emotional clothing pattern, and selecting your clothing personality.

PART II

SIMPLE PRINCIPLES FOR
CONSCIOUS DRESSING

CHAPTER 8

Accessories Make an Outfit

There's no point in trying to look like a Vogue editorial
every month. The way to find your style is to try to
develop a look of your own, something of you,
that people can identify with you.

— Calvin Klein

The Seven Secrets for Expressing the Inner You are all about
learning to express who you are inside — and thus laying the
foundation on which to build your unique wardrobe. Clothing
and fashion tips are fleeting until they can be matched with the
image you have defined for yourself. Only by knowing how you
want to look can you truly create the dressing goddess you have
always wanted to be both inside and out. The Simple Principles
for Conscious Dressing detailed in the next six chapters provide a
how-to for creating a wardrobe that can take you anywhere and
making the dressing process much easier.

So there you are, standing naked in front of your closet, trying to figure out what to wear. Okay, maybe you are not naked,
but still, you are trying to find the right outfit to wear for the
moment, whether you're headed to a corporate meeting, a dinner
party with friends, or a birthday dinner with your boyfriend or
husband. As you embark on the process of learning to look great
in clothes, be aware that you are always designing a look. Instead
of focusing on exactly what to wear, focus on how you want to
look. This shift in thought process takes you from getting dressed
to putting outfits together. This is what looking "put together,"

where every part of your attire contributes to a singular and flattering look, is all about. This is the first principle of conscious dressing: accessories make an outfit.

The right accessory items (handbag, jewelry, shoes) take you from merely putting on clothing to designing and coordinating the perfect outfit. Fashion insiders know this concept well. A great pair of earrings and the perfect handbag can make slacks or jeans and any top, including a T-shirt, look chic instead of just casual. Pulling off this kind of personal look with a minimum of anxiety comes down to two words: attitude and accessories.

Think back to a time when you really felt put together and had the confidence that comes naturally with that feeling. How did you look? What were you wearing and why? I always feel great when I'm dressed up for some party or special event, wearing the right shoes, matching handbag, and the perfect earrings. A cherry-red silk cocktail dress with spaghetti straps and a low V-neck front fitted through the waist with added accessories — fishnet stockings, red slip-on heels, red satin clutch, and cherry-red chandelier earrings, for example — all allow me to feel my put-together best for a holiday party. At such times, I know I look good. Better yet, I feel great about myself. When dressing for a special event, most of us take the time and make the effort to put an outfit together. We add accessory items to design a complete clothing look and image. By applying the same thought process to everyday dressing, you can look put together all the time. The trick is to add at least two to three accessory items to every outfit. This creates a complete clothing look. It's the secret that can expand your current wardrobe tenfold and make you look fantastic consistently.

Take a new look at some of the most commonly worn accessory items. Worn right, they can make an outfit.

HANDBAGS

The right handbag will take you anywhere and dress up anything you are wearing whether it is cargo pants and a pullover cardigan or an evening gown. Handbags are a fashion statement and speak volumes about your clothing style. While they have a practical purpose, they are also a key accessory that can scale a clothing look up or down. You won't catch a Socialite without her designer bag of the season — a Louis Vuitton Murakami bag, for example. She will always use a designer bag to complete her image and clothing look.

There are many fantastic handbags. Some are reasonably priced at less than $50 and other bags are more expensive — from $100 to over $1,000 for name designer bags. Name designer handbags are an investment in your wardrobe if you decide to make it. Designer bags are quality items and will last you virtually forever, so you'll want to choose prudently and look for items that won't quickly pass out of vogue. A small Louis Vuitton clutch can cost anywhere from $165 to over $600, with other bag styles costing from approximately $215 to over $1,000. Christian Dior bags usually start at $210 and go up from there to over $1,000. Gucci, Chanel, and Fendi bags are priced comparably to Louis Vuitton and Christian Dior. Coach, Kate Spade, and Dooney & Bourke offer bags starting at approximately $100, with most bags priced in the $150 to $350 price range. These are only a sampling of designers and costs may vary. Of course handbags that are not designer brands can cost less than $50 in some cases or more than $100 in other cases. It is best to know what you are looking for. Most clothing stores and clothing designers, if not all manufacturers, offer handbags for sale; Jimmy Choo, the shoe designer, for example, also offers for sale a select number of handbags. If there is a clothing store or designer you like, consider looking at their bags, even Gap, known for casual, easy-to-wear clothing, offers great handbags at low prices, usually less than $50. If you buy a handbag that happens to be all the rage one season, just make sure you love it so much and it works so well with your wardrobe that even if it goes out of style, you will still love wearing it. Designer bags are great but you can still look fantastic without the brand name.

Handbags should fit your personal clothing style; that is, does the bag you're considering reflect your personality? A satchel with Indian beading will create a very different effect than a silk clutch. An Actress Type might feel most comfortable with a designer bag because it stands out, or she may select a handbag that has unusual features, from color to beads to little bows regardless of brand. The bag should look hip, possibly a Christian Dior red leather tote or a no-name white wicker tote for day and for evening a Badgley Mischka small, pink satin, round-handle beaded bag or a no name small, black velvet bucket bag with black velvet roses. The Classic Type would probably choose a bag that can stand the test of time, a Louis Vuitton Alma handbag or a simple no-name black clutch. The Artist Type could wear many styles of bags, but if she is wearing a very colorful outfit her bag should be somewhat understated so as not to clash. If her clothing is understated then a colorful bag such as a bright green Balenciaga shoulder bag may be in order, or a no-name colorfully embroidered satchel. Here are some important things to consider when buying a handbag:

+ Do you absolutely love it?

+ Can you can wear it with many outfits (it's an everyday bag) or very few outfits (it is special in color or style, thereby limiting its wearing)?

+ Is it unique so that it really stands out to show how creative you are?

+ Is it a bag of quality you can use forever (designer item)?

+ Does it match an outfit you own exactly (evening wear)?

Use handbags to show your creative flair. The key to choosing the right one is to pick a bag that speaks directly to you and that you will enjoy carrying in many situations. Here are some bag styles to consider: a clutch is great for an evening out, a small tote is perfect for running around town or a casual day out, a messenger bag is great for carrying papers or a computer and works well for the Sporty Type, and a large canvas tote is perfect for the market or beach.

Choose a bag that fits your body type; a bag should help to focus attention away from what you feel are your problem areas. For example, if you have a pear-shaped figure (hips wider than shoulders) avoid carrying a bag that falls off the shoulders and lands on the hips, making them appear wider. Instead, select a bag that hangs between the shoulder and the waist. This will draw attention upward away from the hips. A woman with a straight up and down body can carry a messenger bag with the strap across the body and look good. The same look would not be flattering for a woman with a pear-shaped body or a rounded figure.

The size of a bag is another important consideration. If you have a rounded body, you may want to stay away from a large bag because it will make you look wider and will be less flattering when worn off the shoulder. Petite women can wear oversized bags and not look out of proportion. Bag size should always be evaluated relative to body type.

JEWELRY

Jewelry isn't just for special events and dressing up. Many of us have lovely jewelry but we get lazy and don't put it on. Don't underestimate its power to add just the right finishing touch to your outfit. Jewelry is one of the most personal and expressive fashion statements we can make. It shows off your personality through the kind of materials and design you choose: romantic, vintage, traditional, or modern. Select jewelry that completes your outfit and enhances the overall effect you are aiming for; don't be overly concerned if it is costume or real.

You may also use jewelry to express your personal style in the work environment, but be sure to avoid dangling bracelets or too many of them that may get in that way of your work or annoy others. Choose items such as watches, earrings, or a necklace that show off your style and fit in the office environment.

The following are some important tips for selecting and wearing jewelry:

✦ Select costume jewelry that you love and that will stand out.

✦ Select at least one pair of earrings that can be worn well with everything, and make them a staple of your wardrobe.

✦ Take good care of your jewelry: real jewelry should be regularly and properly cleaned.

✦ Let jewelry reflect the outfit you are wearing and the

mood you are in. For example, a vintage brooch reflects a romantic, artsy mood and an antique necklace may reflect a more old-time conservative flair. Modern jewelry may reflect a cutting-edge mood.

✦ A necklace should complement the neckline and the style of the blouse being worn. A V-neck style blouse, for instance, can really show off a long necklace.

✦ Choose jewelry that shows off your best assets. A long, graceful neck looks great with a choker; women with shorter necks do better with a longer necklace that focuses attention on the bustline. You may also want to match a choker with a long necklace for a more interesting look.

✦ As with sunglasses, select earrings that are opposite the shape of the face. For example, women with round faces should avoid big round earrings and wear dangling earrings to elongate the face. Women with rectangular faces look well with hoop earrings but should avoid square or angled earrings.

✦ Coordinate or mix metals — gold with gold or silver. Also mix with pearls. When mixing metals, try to match the tone and shine of pieces. This will maintain the overall look of the outfit.

✦ Combine a brooch or pins with denim to add style and flair to a casual look.

Invest in gold and/or silver hoop earrings, a watch, and bangle bracelets as wardrobe must-haves. If you feel hoop earrings do not look good on you, buy dangling earrings. As noted above, earrings can do a lot to accentuate your facial features. Choose a style that is right for you: chandelier earrings look great on most faces regardless of shape. They draw attention to the face and upper body and are even more flattering if the colors selected highlight your facial features. As described in chapter 10, women with warm complexions can wear and look good in gold jewelry; silver, platinum, and white gold complement women that have cool complexions.

Rings, watches, and bracelets are other jewelry items that can add style to your outfits. Choose size accordingly. Large items are great but if they are too oversized, they can look out of place on a small hand. The reverse is true for women with large hands: small items may look out of place. Watches are fun and can be decorative. They come in many different face shapes to complement any outfit: round, oval, square, or rectangular. Wear the right jewelry and you will command attention.

SUNGLASSES

Sunglasses aren't worn simply to protect your eyes anymore — they make a statement and add spark to any outfit. Some sunglass manufacturers are known for the quality of their lenses and their ability to block out damaging sun rays. Quality lenses provide 100 percent UV protection and block damaging ultraviolet radiation from your eyes. Always ask to make sure that your eyes are protected.

When choosing sunglasses based on lenses, you should know that there are three major types of sunglass lenses: glass, polycarbonate, and plastic. Glass lenses are heavier and may be more expensive. Today, most lenses are made out of polycarbonate. They are tougher than plastic, and are good for outdoor activities. Plastic lenses are generally less expensive.

Stylish sunglasses can put the final touch on a great outfit. Below are four steps for selecting the right sunglasses for you:

1. Decide the most important factor in your sunglass selection — frames or quality lenses? Many sunglasses provide a little of both.

2. Sunglasses should reflect your personal style. Choose sunglasses that can go with many types of outfits, whether casual or dressy.

3. As with clothing color, make sure the tint and frame color complement your facial features, specifically your skin tone. Choose colors that contrast with your skin tone. If you have a lot of pink in your underlying skin tone, move away from pink tints or frames.

4. Sunglasses should complement the shape of your face. Try
    on a lot of styles to figure out what is right for you.

Here are some tips for selecting sunglasses appropriate to the shape
of your face. As a general rule, to flatter the facial shape, choose
sunglasses whose shapes are counter to that of the face. For example, round-shaped faces are complemented by frames that have
angles; a woman with a round-shaped face might want to consider
glasses with square frames, as this style would downplay the fullness of her face.

A woman with a heart-shaped face should consider frames that
minimize the upper part of the face. Most frame shapes work well
with this type of face. Consider square, rectangular, or heavy-
rimmed frames.

A woman with an oval-shaped face should select frames that
are only as wide as the widest part of the face. Cat-eye sunglass
frames work well.

A woman with a square-shaped face should select frames with
angular shapes. Look for styles that elongate the face. Aviator sunglasses work well.

Most clothing and accessory designers offer a wide selection of
sunglass styles to choose from. When selecting a style, consider
how the sunglasses will fit on the bridge of the nose. Make sure
they lie right on the face.

GLASSES

If you wear glasses for vision correction, rather than contacts,
choose frames that fit your personal style and complement the
shape of your face, as explained above. What image would you like
to create? How would you like others to view you — for instance,
as an intellectual or creative type? Glasses can create any image.
Aviator glasses, made famous in the 1970s, or 1950s-style heavy rim
glasses are just two options for adding creative flair to your choices
of glasses or sunglasses. Buy more than one pair for different looks
and styles; mix it up a little bit. Colored contact lenses are also
fun and add a little spice to your overall look.

SHOES

I don't know who invented the high heel, but all men owe a lot to him.

— Marilyn Monroe

Casual and dress shoes: As every woman knows, shoes complete any outfit. They can make your outfit look finished or end up making it look unfinished. A crystal beaded chiffon slipdress with white slip-on mules may look unfinished or dressed down; pair the same dress with crystal-trimmed, high heel, ankle strap sandals and you are ready for your girlfriend's party. I love shoes. No matter how many pairs I own, I am always able to find one more pair that I need. They are fun to wear and can make an outfit look sexy, casual, and seriously awesome. A simple black minidress is no longer simple if paired with Manolo Blahnik black heels that lace up the calves with satin ribbons, or a silver minidress by Nicole Miller can be paired with metallic Stuart Weitzman strappy stilettos for a perfectly coordinated look. A business suit looks great with pumps purchased from an Arthur Beren store or an Armani suit looks sexy when paired with a Giuseppe Zanotti design.

If you are going to wear open-toed shoes or mules, be sure your feet and nails are well groomed. Mules are a must for your wardrobe — they go nicely with jeans and can subtly add height if you are short.

Six characteristics of well-chosen shoes are:

✦ They complete many outfits.

✦ They add height if you are feeling short (always a great pick-me-up).

✦ They fit well and comfortably. High heel shoes may not be comfortable at times but they are endured in the name of fashion. Shoe designer Taryn Rose makes shoes that are stylish and comfortable at the same time, a match that at times is hard to find. Match comfort level to how long you will be wearing the shoe. If you are going to be walking a lot, take that into account. If you are wearing high heels to a dinner party when you will be sitting down or mingling most of the night, then you may be able to withstand any discomfort that may arise from looking fabulous.

✦ They should get noticed because they accentuate what you are wearing.

✦ They match your personal style (sexy, casual, and sporty).

✦ You absolutely love them!

As with handbags, there are many great shoe designers: Giuseppe Zanotti, Jimmy Choo, Stuart Weitzman, Christian Louboutin, and Manolo Blahnik — as well as many stores that offer great shoe designs that may be less costly than the above-named designers: Charles David, Nine West, and Steve Madden, for example. Big department stores (such as Nordstrom, Bloomingdale's, Barney's New York, Saks Fifth Avenue, Bergdorf Goodman, Neiman Marcus, and Macy's) have great shoe departments with a wide selection of shoes from both well-known designers and unknown brands. They also offer less expensive brands such as Nina and Via Spiga. Even larger discount stores such as Target, Marshalls, T.J. Maxx, and JCPenney, carry a wide selection of shoes at low prices. Shoes, just like handbags, can cost less than $50 or greater than $1,000. Decide what you want to spend on shoes.

Choose a style of shoe that matches the outfit or clothing look you are trying to achieve. For example, pumps create a different look than strappy sandals and may be more appropriate for office wear.

Tennis shoes can help a sweat outfit look hip, or make shorts and jeans look cool. They can be plain and basic, so long as they are clean. The quickest way to grunge down a casual outfit is to wear dirty tennis shoes. There are plenty of stylish, well-made tennis shoes that serve different purposes. There are workout shoes that can be worn for exercise or just running around, and then there are shoes whose sole purpose is to make you look adorable. Most tennis shoe designers make both kinds of shoes; some are known for the workout shoe, and others are known for sporty shoes for running around looking cute, fun, and hip. Nike, Reebok, and Adidas make workout shoes that are designed in fun, funky styles and colors such as white shoes with orange stripes or black and gray shoes with air pockets. New Balance makes great walking or workout shoes that are less about flash and color and more seriously about giving your foot the best support. Puma makes fun, cutting-edge styles and colors in shoes to run around and look adorable in as well as workout shoes. Vans, Keds, and Skechers are other running-around shoe manufacturers and styles to consider. Tennis shoes can be purchased for design or comfort or a little of both. Cropped red jeans, a blazer, and a silk camisole with heels is great for a dinner with friends but the same outfit worn during the day can look cute and casual if paired with a funky and hip style shoe from Puma, for example.

HAIR ACCESSORIES

Women know that when they're running out of the house and don't have time to do anything with their hair, hair clips always come in handy. Be sure to purchase hair clips that match your hair type: women with fine hair do better with smaller clips that hold their hair without being overbearing. Women with thick hair and lots of it need larger clips with more teeth.

How you wear your hair creates a fashion style in and of itself. The Socialite Type may be seen in a perfectly fitted suit with her hair in an updo for a dinner party. The Classic Type may wear headbands or a simple ponytail. The Artist or Actress Type may be a little more creative wearing her hair in pigtails with a slip-on knit hat. The Rebel Type may be seen with her hair messy with pink dye or spiked out. Some people have the same hairstyle for years and years because for them it creates a fashion statement. A woman who keeps her hair straight all of her life without using hair clips, hats, or other accessories to create different looks may get bored or may miss out on keeping her style fresh. This is why entertainment figures continue to change their looks to keep the public interested. Keeping the same hair look for twenty years doesn't work unless it is your fashion statement, like those of Jacqueline Kennedy Onassis or her sister, Lee Radziwill. Their hairstyles were classic statements of clean lines and simplicity. Know what works for you and be aware of the amount of effort you are willing to dedicate to a hair-style — you'll want to avoid haircuts that do not work for your lifestyle.

HATS

Baseball hats look and work great when you're out running errands; if you didn't have time to wash your hair; they are great to throw on, but they can quickly dress down any outfit.

Below are three factors to consider when buying a hat:

+ Buy hats that will last not only in quality but in style.

+ Make sure to buy the right size hat. Don't let a salesperson talk you into a size because that is all they may have left. Designer hats are usually unisex, meaning they come in the same sizes for both men and women.

+ A hat should complement your facial shape and skin color. Make sure that the hat you choose does not overwhelm your facial features. You want people to notice how great you look, not an oversized hat.

The right hat can make you stand out and create a distinct look. A pink pair of slacks with a black, scrunched-in-the-waist, short sleeve top and black pumps become more glamorous when a pink hat is added to the outfit. A great sheath dress is made to look com-plete with a pillbox hat and is perfect for the Socialite or Classic Type. A beret would change the look of a gathered dress and look great on the Artist or Actress Type.

BELTS

Belts are great if they complement your body type; not everyone can wear belts. Women with rounder figures should stay away from belts because they highlight the midsection of the body. A woman with a straight up and down body type will benefit from wearing a belt because it gives her more of a waist. Thick ornate belts work with low-rise jeans. Coordinate your belts with other accessories. To match gold or silver earrings, try wearing a belt with a matching buckle. Use chain belts wrapped loosely around the waist for a sexy look.

SCARVES/WRAPS

Scarves are a bit like jewelry — a personal touch, a caprice, a vice.

— Georgio Armani

Scarves and wraps are extremely versatile. You can dress up a business suit with a scarf or keep yourself warm by adding a wrap to a dress. You can throw a scarf around your neck for a quick twist to an otherwise simple outfit. Scarves and wraps come in all different shapes, sizes, and fabrics (for example, silk, chiffon, wool, cashmere). Buy wraps and scarves that you will actually wear; more often than not we buy these types of accessory items and rarely think to add them to our outfits as accessories. Before every purchase, ask yourself, "Will I really wear this?" This question will help to eliminate mistaken purchases. Select colors for wraps and scarves that coordinate with your wardrobe and flatter your skin tone. Choose scarves that match your body size — don't let a large scarf overwhelm a petite frame or a small scarf get mismatched with a larger body frame.

Here are eight ideas to consider for wearing accessory items well:

✦   Choose accessories that complete the clothing look you are after. If you are going for a conservative look, don't wear funky earrings. The quickest way to look like you don't know how to dress is to mix and match styles that don't go together, unless of course you are the Rebel personality type and that is your personal style.

Decide on the clothing look you're aiming for, and then coordinate your accessory items to match that look. Here are some ideas: For a classy look, tie a scarf around your neck to dress up any suit or wear it wrapped around your shoulders. For a sexy look, wear dangling crystal earrings with a cashmere skirt and fitted tee. Go funky with a beret, a miniskirt, and cowboy boots. Get dressy in high heel strappy shoes and a lace chiffon dress with diamond earrings. Dress up your casual outfit of khaki pants and jean jacket with a vintage brooch.

✦ Decide what each look means to you. What I think is sexy may be different from what you think is sexy. Our culture and upbringing will have a lot to do with that. Choose your look and then coordinate your accessories to complete your vision.

✦ Choose accessory items that you know you will be comfortable wearing. Looking great in any outfit is about dressing to your comfort level. When we are comfortable with how we look, we are confident. A great scarf with a classic dress is only great if you wear it with confidence.

✦ Choose accessories that don't overwhelm you or your look. For example, taller women can wear oversized accessories without being overwhelmed by them, but for petite women, accessory size does matter.

✦ When in doubt, keep it accessory simple. If you don't know what accessories to wear for a specific outfit, add simple pieces, such as hoop earrings and a tote handbag.

✦ Wear at least two to three accessory items to complete your outfit look. Handbag, earrings, and the right shoes can make your outfit stand out.

✦ Buy accessory items well; make sure they are unique pieces or items you absolutely love. For example, when we wear a handbag we love, we will take pleasure in showing it off, and others will notice how put together we look.

✦ Understand that accessory items do make a statement. What do your accessories say about your personality?

✦ Get creative: your accessory items don't need to look like they came from a museum. Adding a simple black scarf to a top and slacks can change your whole clothing look simply.

ACCESSORY ACTION PLAN

✦ Go through your current accessory items. Give away anything you haven't worn in over a year — including belts, hats, and non-valuable jewelry.

✦ Separate real jewelry from costume jewelry. Keep jewelry in a safe place. Repair jewelry as necessary so that it is readily available to wear.

✦ Review your shoes: throw away or give away shoes that are worn and can't be repaired. Clean and polish shoes and take others to be resoled or repaired if needed.

✦ Make a list of all the accessory items you currently own by category (see chapter 14).

✦ Begin a list of accessory items that you need to add to your wardrobe to complete clothing looks. Then buy them over time as you find items you absolutely must have.

✦ Make sure the accessory items you wear are in line with the clothing look you want to create.

SUMMARY

✦ Use accessory items to create the perfect "put together" look.

✦ Add at lease two to three accessory items to every outfit.

✦ Know the most commonly worn accessory items.

✦ The right handbag can complete any look.

✦ Jewelry allows you to express your own personal style.

✦ Sunglasses make a statement and add spark to any outfit.

✦ Glasses can be used to change your image.

✦ Shoes complete an outfit.

✦ How you wear your hair and the hair accessories you use can create a fashion statement.

✦ The right hat can make you stand out and create a distinctive look.

✦ Belts should complement your body type.

✦ Scarves and wraps are extremely versatile.

CHAPTER 9

Good Quality Never Goes Out of Style

You do not need a lot of clothes. Just buy very well made clothes that are simple and of very good quality.

— Fernando Sanchez

There is so much competing merchandise in the clothing area today. How do you know that what you are buying will stand the test of time and when should this be important? Quality clothing items are considered quality because of the care that goes into them during the manufacturing process. This means that the components that make up the item — hems, seams, zippers, buttons, linings — should be evaluated to determine quality. Is the hem double stitched? Do the zippers work easily? Are there any loose threads in the seams? Is the lining fabric smooth so that the clothing lies nicely? Price does not guarantee quality. How an item is made and the richness of the fabric are ways to determine quality. Quality items are essential to building a wardrobe that can grow with you as your image evolves. This is the second simple principle for conscious dressing: good quality never goes out of style. Not all of your wardrobe items have to be of the highest quality, but key wardrobe items such as jackets, leather items (coats, pants, boots), and fine coats should be.

In the previous chapter we looked at the importance of accessorizing the clothing you choose in assembling complete outfits and creating clothing looks that reflect the beauty self you've defined.

Another way to accessorize is by adding key wardrobe items. Key wardrobe items are any clothing items that accessorize an outfit. They can be worn with differing outfits and make each outfit look complete and unique. Examples of key wardrobe items are coats, jackets, leather goods, vests, and certain significant footwear, including boots.

There are three characteristics that define key wardrobe items:

1. Key wardrobe items can be worn with multiple outfits. For example, a denim jacket can be worn with a red turtleneck, white jeans, loafers, and a white leather bag for one outfit and then be worn over a pink, flowered slipdress and sandals to create another outfit.

2. Key wardrobe items can be made to look dressy or casual depending on the clothes they are being paired with. For example, high heel brown boots worn with jeans and a wrap top can look casual or more than casual if worn with a suede skirt, halter top, and khaki jacket. Then pair the brown boots with a classic double-breasted white skirt suit and a vintage bag to create an even dressier look.

3. Key wardrobe items stay in style over the long term. For example, a trench coat can be worn for many years and still complement every outfit it is paired with.

When you are able to add key wardrobe items to your wardrobe, you expand your choices of outfits without quantity purchasing. Creating your own unique look becomes easy. By adding accessories and key wardrobe items to a basic pair of black pants and a solid or striped T-shirt, you can put together any number of outfits. For example, outfit 1: add a suede jacket in red with red strappy heels to a solid gray, low scoop-neck tee to create a funky dressed-up look; outfit 2: add a pashmina wrap in green to a black boatneck long sleeve tee with black boots and a retro bag; outfit 3: combine a pink scrunchy tee with a fuchsia blazer and pink platform heels; and outfit 4: mix a black and white striped short sleeve tee with a bomber jacket and bucket bag.

Think about the important clothing and accessory items you own. What key wardrobe items might you want to acquire to

GOOD QUALITY NEVER GOES out of STYLE

101

expand your wardrobe to create multiple clothing looks? Here are some examples of quality key wardrobe items (the items in italics are the key wardrobe items):

✦ A beautifully tailored brown *leather jacket* can be worn with a sundress during the day to create a funkier look and that same jacket can be worn with an A-line skirt, pumps, a velvet-trimmed top, and open-toed high heel shoes for an evening out.

✦ A *peacoat* can be worn during the day over a short skirt and tall suede boots along with a fitted V-neck pullover sweater and a saddle bag. The same peacoat can be used to dress up blue and white striped menswear trousers and a silk halter worn with Prada *mules* at night.

✦ A black pair of *high heel* boots can be worn with a pencil skirt and a jean jacket. The *boots* can be worn with casual clothing or a dark suit.

✦ A suede *pantsuit* can be worn for a dressy night out or a lunch with girlfriends and can be paired with multiple tops and different shoes and bags to create more than one clothing look.

When we buy key wardrobe items of quality, we build a wardrobe that lasts and will take us through many fashion seasons. Here are some characteristics of quality key wardrobe items:

✦ Quality key wardrobe items are well made, or at least look well made.

✦ Quality key wardrobe items can stand the test of time. They look new no matter how many times they are worn.

✦ Key wardrobe items complete the overall look of an outfit.

✦ Quality items fit well; there are no extra puckers in the fabric or loose threads sticking out.

✦ Quality key wardrobe items increase a wardrobe tenfold with each purchase.

When choosing quality items, keep in mind the following three guidelines:

✦ *Always choose quality over buying in quantity for key wardrobe pieces.* As described above, a key wardrobe piece is any significant clothing item that accessorizes an outfit. Buying clothing items in quantity does not necessarily mean we have more to wear. Many times we end up having too many of the wrong clothing choices.

✦ *Select the level of quality necessary for an item you are thinking of buying based on what it is and how often you are likely to be wearing it.* For example, if you are purchasing a white T-shirt, is it important to buy a high quality white T-shirt? Only if it is unique or it is an integral part of your fashion statement. The point is that when choosing how to spend your money, the level of quality is relative to how it is going to be valued by you. When you build a wardrobe, it is best to spend more money on key wardrobe items of quality (jackets, boots) that you can have for the long term than on more minor clothing items that will fade after a couple of washes.

✦ *Select quality items that are unique and timeless.* When you are buying a quality clothing item, ask yourself, "Can I see myself wearing this through many fashion seasons?" or "Can I wear this to complete many outfits?" Make sure your key wardrobe items are unique enough to show off your personality and personal style.

Quality items should fit your body type. A quality item that fits your body type will show that you know how to dress to reflect your own inner image. If you love an item and it doesn't fit right, it will never fit right and it will never look right on you. Here are some additional points to consider when selecting quality key wardrobe items:

✦ *Make sure that clothing and key wardrobe items fit well.* We have all bought clothing that is too tight, hoping to change our body shape later on. There are so many clothing choices that can make us look great today, it makes much more sense to buy what fits right now, instead of something that is too big or too small. You don't want to add an unworn item to your closet and then have to give it away later.

+ *Evaluate clothing fabric to determine longevity.* The type of fabric you are purchasing will determine how your clothing items will wear over time and how they will look through many washes and wears. Silk, linen, wool, and cotton are natural fabrics and rayon, polyester, and nylon are man-made fabrics. Cotton items will typically shrink when washed and silk, linen, wool, and rayon usually have to be dry-cleaned and are therefore more expensive to take care of. The type of fabric or leather you are buying will affect how you will need to take care of the item and the costs associated with that care.

+ *Evaluate workmanship.* When you buy clothes of either high or low quality, it is important to factor in workmanship relative to the cost of the clothing item. If you are buying a ten-dollar pair of pants, you may not expect perfect stitching, but it is essential on expensive, high quality items. Check for loose threads, make sure buttons are sewn on right, and look for puckers in the material to make sure it lies flat.

Beautiful suits or suit jackets to wear for work or evenings out should fit well with clean lines and good quality workmanship. Not every suit has to be of high quality but you should have at least one high quality suit jacket to dress up work clothes or add to a skirt and blouse for an evening out.

In order to figure out what key clothing items you need to complement and complete your wardrobe, you will need to know what you own (see chapter 14). Your key quality clothing items, such as coats, blazers, and boots, should complement what you already own and provide depth to your wardrobe, creating flexibility and allowing you to mix and match other clothing pieces more easily.

When you have bought your quality wardrobe pieces, will you know how to take care of them? Taking good care of your clothes is just as important as buying quality items in the first place. Here are some good suggestions for wardrobe upkeep:

+ After wearing, always hang up and put away your clothes.

+ Clean garments when they are dirty — don't wait.

+ To clean, follow garment labels.

+ Organize accessory items. Keep jewelry clean.

+ Protect leather and suede items, following label instructions for special cleaning.

+ Reheel or resole shoes as needed.

Quality clothing items are essential for building a wardrobe. Consider this: Kimberly has been building a wardrobe since she was eighteen years old. When she went shopping with her best friend, Sari, the latter often bought at least three less expensive clothing items for the same money that Kimberly spent on one high fashion coat. Five years later, Kimberly still has and wears her coat. Her friend Sari no longer has many of her purchases and is still buying clothing that becomes worn-out after a short period of time. Quality wardrobe items are essential to making the dressing process easy.

SUMMARY

+ Key wardrobe items are any clothing items that accessorize an outfit (jackets, boots, coats, leather items). Go through your closet and determine how many key wardrobe items you own.

+ Determine what key wardrobe items you need to buy to fill in your wardrobe gaps.

+ Buy quality instead of quantity for key wardrobe items.

✦ Know the three factors for selecting quality key wardrobe items.

✦ Take proper care of your clothing and quality key wardrobe items.

✦ Learn to mix and match quality items for a complete fashion statement.

CHAPTER 10

Color Coordinate Your Wardrobe

Color is like food for the spirit —
plus it is not addicting or fattening.

— Isaac Mizrahi

Principle Three — color coordinate — makes putting together outfits easy. Before I knew better, whenever I went shopping I just bought whatever I thought looked good on me, regardless of color or whether it fit with the rest of my wardrobe. I wasn't really assembling a wardrobe, I was impulse buying. I would buy funky prints or unusual colors and then when I went to wear them, I found that I had nothing to wear with them. Have you had the same experience? The principles for conscious dressing can help you learn to reduce or eliminate these kinds of mistaken purchases. Principle Three shows you how to select only clothing in colors that fit within your wardrobe color scheme.

By color coordinating your wardrobe, you can eliminate the guesswork when trying on clothing and trying to figure out which color to buy a given item in. For example, if you are about to buy a purple sweater, make sure that purple is a color you have chosen as part of your color-coordinated wardrobe. How do you color coordinate a wardrobe?

The best way to color coordinate your wardrobe is to:

1.   select your signature color;

2. pick two to three secondary colors;

3. intersperse black and white into your wardrobe as needed.

Most of us have a lot of black in our wardrobe. Black and white work with any color scheme you choose. You can always add new items of clothing in white or black to the colors in your wardrobe. Black is easy because it slenderizes and goes with everything, but clothing creativity is lost when we wear black all the time. The quickest way to perk up an outfit and look beautiful is to add color.

Color makes us beautiful and bright and feminine. It allows us to stand out and show off who we are. It accentuates our skin tone and facial features. A black suit with a pink top is much more attractive than a black suit with a black top. A Classic Type can spruce up her wardrobe by adding color without changing her clothing style, for instance, by purchasing a sheath dress in mauve. Then she can add a mauve sweater tossed over her shoulders and tied around her neck with mauve sling back shoes.

Try the following: add one brightly colored clothing item to any outfit and see how your clothing self changes. Add a red scarf to a black pantsuit or brighten up those white slacks by adding a lime-green vintage jacket. Then, for at least one day, do not wear anything black. How does this make you feel?

When you first try this, you may feel uncomfortable, not sure whether you look good in colors or are dressed appropriately. This is especially true if you are not used to standing out, or prefer not to be noticed. As an alternative to bright-colored clothing, choose pastels for a more subtle look. With practice, you'll find that adding color to your outfits adds a level of interest and creativity to the dressing process. Looking back to the exercises in chapter 1, when you defined your image, what colors came to mind when imagining the perfect clothing you? When you looked through magazines for the picture of the clothing look you liked, what colors stood out?

Colors are perfect for brightening your mood when you are feeling down or low on energy. If you are tired, add color to what you wear. Notice how the brightness of your clothing revitalizes you. Many times when we are tired, we choose dark colors that reflect that mood. Next time you're feeling a bit low and about to don a dark outfit, make the effort to choose clothing colors that are opposite your mood, and see how much better they make you feel — and look.

What is a signature color? A signature color is the one you most like to wear, which also complements your facial features — eyes, skin tone, and hair color. Your signature color can be paired favorably with two to three secondary colors to create a color-coordinated wardrobe.

How do you pick a signature color and how do you select secondary colors? There are three factors to consider when selecting your wardrobe colors:

✦ Facial features: most important, eyes, skin tone, and hair color

✦ Comfort level

✦ Current wardrobe

You should be comfortable wearing the colors you choose, and they should coordinate with your current wardrobe, unless you are building a new wardrobe from scratch.

Flattering colors should make your eyes stand out, complement your hair color, and highlight your skin tone. The wrong clothing colors can actually make you appear less attractive than you are. Ideally, your clothing should show off your beauty and make people notice your face. Colors can change the way you appear quicker than any clothing style — just ask any woman who colors her hair (and I do).

Changing your hair color can also change what clothing colors look best on you. For instance, the wrong shade of blonde for my hair color will make me look ten years older, while the right shade makes me look fabulous. When I lightened my hair, I had to adjust my wardrobe colors just slightly so as not to look washed-out. Just as hair color affects the way we look, so too does clothing color.

Colors impact our image and each color sends a message. Here are some examples of colors and the messages they send:

+ *Bright colors such as red, purple, bright green, or yellow say, "I am energetic, confident, and extroverted."*

+ *Dark colors such as dark navy and black say, "I am an authority and I am credible."* This is why professional women wear blue or black suits especially in business.

+ *Lighter colors such as pink and other pastels say, "I am feminine."* This is why many women like to wear pink.

+ *Warm colors such as light beige, camel, and off-white say, "I am friendly and down-to-earth."* This is why the Sporty Type clothing personality likes to wear beiges and light-colored casual clothing.

+ *Cool colors such as light blue say, "I am classic and conservative."*

The colors you select for your wardrobe will reflect your personality, and the personality type described in chapter 2 that most fits you should link up with the colors you choose for your wardrobe. For example, if you like to stand out (the Actress personality type) you will be likely to choose brighter colors to wear. If you like to be more defiant (the Rebel personality type) you will probably choose darker colors such as black and red to wear.

As noted above, the first step in selecting the right colors for your wardrobe is finding those that complement your skin tone. To do this, you need to identify your underlying complexion. There are two types of underlying skin tone complexions: warm and cool. Women with warm complexions have yellow, peach, or red in the underlying tone of their skin. If you have a warm complexion you will generally look better in colors such as dark brown, camel, yellow-green, red-orange, and blues. *As a rule, if you look better in beige than in white, you probably have a warm complexion.*

Women with cool complexions have pink, violet, or blue in their underlying skin tone. If you have a cool complexion you will generally look better in colors such as pink, blue-green, black, white, and burgundy. *As a rule, if you look better in white than in beige, you probably have a cool complexion.*

The cool and warm complexion categories are basic guidelines for clothing color selection. There may be times when you can pull off wearing colors from either category. This is just a way to help you begin to get an idea of which colors look best on you based on your skin tone.

Warm and cool complexions can be more specifically categorized by a process known as "selecting your season." This usually involves professional image consultants, who can analyze the best color palette for you personally. They can tell you what colors look best on you based on your skin tone, hair color, and overall look. Each color grouping is named after a season: summer, spring, autumn, and winter. Summer and winter fall into the cool complexion category (pink, violet, or blue underlying skin tone). Spring and autumn fall into the warm complexion category (yellow, peach, and red underlying skin tone). When you have your colors professionally analyzed, the consultant will provide you with an individualized color palette of various shades from which you should choose for your clothes and makeup to complement your features. If you would like a more detailed analysis of the colors that are right for you personally, there are many books solely on this topic, or you may want to contact a color or image consultant.

Some of us have already selected colors for our wardrobe. My girlfriend's signature color is pink. She likes the feminine look, and the color looks great with her underlying skin tone, which is also pink, i.e., the cool complexion category. I have a warm complexion and can't wear certain pink tones. I look better in blue tones.

Once you select your signature color, the next step toward a color-coordinated wardrobe is to select two to three secondary colors that you can attractively combine with your signature color. These colors should also look good with your personal coloring and complement your current wardrobe. For example, I am blonde with blue eyes. I selected wardrobe colors that maximized what I already had in my wardrobe and matched my skin tone (warm). My signature color is blue because it makes my eyes sparkle and stand out. I selected camel (brown tones) and yellow as my secondary colors. All of the colors I selected can be color coordinated: camel looks good with brown, blue looks good with camel, yellow looks great with blue. Then I intersperse black and white into my wardrobe as needed.

Once you have selected your colors, shopping becomes much easier. You buy clothing in the colors you have selected. You can always buy outside of your color scheme if you fall in love with a clothing item or a color such as red for the holidays. Clothing in solid or patterned materials can work: I have brown patterned tops that I can wear with camel pants or a yellow top I can combine with jeans and a blue blazer.

MY COLOR-COORDINATED WARDROBE   **COLORS COMBINED**

1. Blue   (Black)   Blue-Camel-Yellow

2. Camel/Brown   (White)   Yellow-Blue

3. Yellow   Camel-Black

YOUR COLOR COORDINATED WARDROBE   **COLORS COMBINED**

1. _____   (Black)   _____-_____

2. _____   (White)   _____-_____

3. _____   _____-_____

The color coordination of your wardrobe makes creating multiple outfits easy even with a limited amount of clothing, through mixing and matching. If everything in your wardrobe fits together as part of the same color scheme, you will no longer have to say, "What can I wear with that orange skirt?"

SUMMARY

+ Choosing a signature color and secondary colors allows you to color coordinate your wardrobe and make the dressing process simple.

+ Colors can alter your mood and affect the way you see yourself.

✦ Your color choices should make your eyes, hair, and skin look fabulous and coordinate with clothing you already own.

✦ Identifying your skin tone type will help you choose your signature color.

CHAPTER 11

Know Your Body

Fashion is architecture: It is a matter of proportions.
— Gabrielle "Coco" Chanel

Becky has an hourglass body shape with a small waist, an ample chest, and a round behind. She has been wearing fitted clothing that has not been the most flattering for her. At times she finds her clothing riding up on her or pulling down in the bust line. Becky wants to learn to dress better for her body type. What should she wear? For an hourglass or curvy shape, instead of fitted clothing from head to toe, clothing should be worn that accentuates the waist. A dress that is fitted through the waist and flares out slightly minimizes the roundness in the lower half of Becky's body while drawing attention to her small waist. Wrap dresses, such as the one made famous by Diane von Furstenberg, work very well for this type of body. Also consider suit jackets that cinch in at the waist. This type of figure should avoid square-cut jackets. Lighter material will typically be more flattering than heavier material that may add width to this body type.

The key to buying the right clothes is knowing what kind of clothes fit your specific body type. The first three principles in this section have shown you how to create complete clothing looks by adding accessories and key wardrobe items to every outfit, and by color coordinating your wardrobe. Now let's explore the importance of knowing what clothing fits your specific body type for the most flattering look.

Too many times we misguidedly buy and wear clothes that do not accentuate our positive body features. We may buy clothes that look good on someone else and then wonder why they don't look great on us. Understanding what clothing styles and materials look best on you increases your clothing confidence tenfold and, like all the principles in this section, makes knowing what to wear easier.

To start selecting clothing based on your body type, you must identify the following:

1. Body Type. *How you are physically proportioned?*

2. Best Body Features. *What makes you stand out?*

Let's look at each factor in more detail.

BODY TYPE

Understanding your body type is about analyzing your body specifically, learning what kinds of clothing flatter it best, and then deciding what you are comfortable wearing. Your body can be viewed like a T. The T represents your body type evaluated by length and width. The length is how your body is proportioned upward. The width is how you are shaped in the bust, waist, and hips.

Each factor should be considered when deciding what clothing will look best on you.

Length Proportion

How you are proportioned in length may be divided into two sections as follows:

✦ head to hips

✦ hips to toes

Understanding which part of your body is longer or shorter is important because it allows you to decide which part of your body to highlight and which to play down. We have no control over how we are proportioned vertically. We cannot make ourselves taller or change the length of our waist, but we can maximize our beauty potential by learning to dress according to those proportions. Most women do not take into account how their bodies are proportioned upward and because of this, they are not able to dress to best fit their own body type. A woman with a longer upper body will look her best wearing different clothing than a woman with a longer lower body and longer legs even if these women have the same width shape in the hips, bust, and waist.

Is the upper half of your body (measured from hips up) longer than the lower half of the body, or is the lower half of your body (measured from the hips down) longer? Or are you perfectly proportioned vertically (equal halves)? Knowing the answers to these questions will help you to use the dressing tips below:

+ *Always choose clothing that highlights the longest part of your body.* For example, if you have a longer lower body relative to your upper body (i.e., long legs), highlight your lower body. Take the focus away from your upper body by directing the eyes downward. Wear longer jackets to balance your longer legs and avoid high-waisted clothing.

+ *If you have shorter legs, you may appear to be shorter than you really are.* As in tip 1, wear clothing that highlights the longest part of your body, in this case your upper body. Wear short jackets and high-waisted clothing to make yourself appear taller. Focus on the upper body by directing the eyes upward.

+ *If your body is somewhat proportional (lower half equals upper half), you can wear many different clothing styles.*

+ *Always choose fitted clothes regardless of your proportions.* Fitted clothes highlight your best body features. Loose-fitting clothing may make you appear bigger than you are. Clothing that is too tight will show every flaw.

Width Frame

Many fashion books and magazines describe the different body types — pear-shaped, hourglass, full-busted — to refer to your horizontal frame. Are your hips wider than your bust or is your bust bigger than your hips? What is your waist size? Many women already know whether they are pear-shaped, hourglass, or straight up and down. The key to dressing your width frame is to try to balance out your body shape. Below are some ideas on how to do that for each body type.

PEAR-SHAPED BODY Hips are wider than shoulders, the bust is small. Weight is carried on the lower part of the body. Some petite women may also have this body type. Any time the upper body is smaller than the lower body you will most likely have a pear-shaped body.

+ To balance this body type, add weight to the upper body and shoulders so that they appear wider. Wear full blouses that gather at the shoulder and force vision upward. Top styles to look for are boatnecks and cowl-necks.

+ Tops should never end mid-thigh or at the widest part of the hip. Instead wear fitted tops that end anywhere that will not cut the vision of a straight body line.

+ Avoid wearing heavy fabric or patterns below the waist; keep fabric on the lower body simple with lighter material such as rayon.

+ Use jewelry to focus attention upward and to the face, such as dangling or chandelier earrings.

V-SHAPED BODY Shoulders are wider than hips, hips are narrow. Weight is carried on the upper part of the body. This is what is sometimes referred to as top-heavy. Women with V-shaped bodies have bigger busts or in some cases have very broad shoulders and medium busts.

+ To balance the look of a V-shaped body, you must add emphasis to the hips. This can be done by wearing patterned or textured fabric below the waist or any fabric with a heavier material such as brocade or velvet. The key here is to focus vision downward to balance this body type.

✦ Avoid patterned and textured tops on the upper body. Tops in lightweight fabric such as silk are ideal because they do not widen the upper body.

✦ Keep accessories close to the face so as not to widen the upper body.

HOURGLASS BODY Here, hips and shoulders are balanced, and the waist is small. Weight is carried equally on the top and bottom.

✦ A woman with this type of body should show off her waist. Wraps and belts are great ways to do this.

✦ Emphasize the waist and shape through soft, flowing material. Avoid bulky material as it adds width.

✦ Wear one color from head to toe for an elongated look.

STRAIGHT UP AND DOWN BODY Hips and shoulders are balanced; waist is undefined or average to large.

✦ To balance this body type, try to make the waist look smaller so that the body shape appears more defined. Avoid boxy clothing and stiff fabrics.

✦ Wear clothing that elongates the body including V-neck tops. Belts work well for this body type.

✦ Jewelry and scarves work well because they focus attention on the neckline.

✦ Look for clothing items that are made of a softer fabric in styles that add curves. Items that gather or have ruffles create a more feminine frame.

ROUNDED BODY Hips and shoulders are balanced, waist full, bust may or may not be full.

✦ Wear long tops and sweaters to avoid highlighting the waist.

✦ The same color of clothing on the top and bottom will flatter this body type.

✦ Wear long jackets over shorter straight skirts.

✦ Avoid clothing that is too tight across the middle or fabrics that are unforgiving and highlight every bulge.

✦ Choose fabrics that are flowing but still fit the body shape.

Understanding the two body type factors will enable you to identify your body type and give you a better idea of the clothing you need to buy to fit it. Too often we focus on the size of our hips or bust, or how much we weigh to determine what we should wear when we also need to take into account our upward proportion. If a woman is big-busted and has long legs, she needs to select different clothing styles than those a woman who is big-busted with a shorter lower body should wear. Each woman should highlight the longest part of her body. One woman will highlight her lower body and the other woman will highlight her upper body. Clothing styles will flatter each of these women differently.

The best way to get to know your body type is to go shopping and try on clothes. Try spending a day alone or with friends shopping just to try on clothes. Try on different types and styles of clothing with the information you've learned in this chapter in mind, until you begin to understand what works for your body type.

At the same time, you have to figure out what you are comfortable wearing. At a certain point in my life I could have easily worn fitted clothing, as my body type is somewhat proportioned, but I wasn't comfortable enough with myself to do that. I didn't know how to handle the attention, so instead of becoming more confident, I played myself down. I didn't dress to my potential. Our comfort level in choosing what to wear is linked to our personality type (chapter 2). Two women with similar hourglass-shaped bodies will make different clothing choices based on their personality type, which drives their comfort level. For example, an Actress personality type with an hourglass shape may choose for an evening out to wear a bright green beaded satin dress fitted through the waist that flares slightly and has an uneven hemline. She could pair it with a green envelope clutch, stiletto heels, and a sheer wrap. Her personality type is about standing out, so this would fit her comfort level. This outfit may not work for a Classic Type who has an hourglass figure. She may be more comfortable with a simple black halter dress that accentuates the waist, black pumps, diamond stud earrings and a cashmere coat.

Another example of how dressing for your body type is influenced by your clothing personality: A woman with a straight up and down body who classifies herself as the Sporty Type may wear, for a casual evening out, beige fitted pants cropped with a pink V-neck silk camisole, a rhinestone belt, a fitted short suit jacket, and mules. She could wear the same outfit for a casual errand-running day just by replacing the silk camisole with a tank top, adding a brown belt, and wearing a jean jacket instead of the suit jacket. If she fits the Classic Type instead of the Sporty Type, she would wear something like black slacks, a black silk button-down blouse, a black belt, sling back heels, and a pink sweater tossed over her shoulders with a pink handbag to match. Body type drives the styles of clothing that flatter the body. In this example both women, as dictated by their body type, wear tops that elongate the body and belts to make the waist look smaller, but the clothing each chooses is determined also by her personality and hence her comfort level.

Once you know your body specifically, you will understand the types and styles of clothing that are the most flattering for you. Your clothing personality will then influence how those styles are worn and in what colors and fabrics.

EXERCISE
BEST BODY FEATURES

What are your best body features? Do you have a small waist? Do you have a big bust? Do you have a small bust? Do you have a heart-shaped behind? Do you have great legs? Do you have a cut stomach? Do you have toned, muscular arms? Do you have a great back? Every one of us has at least one positive body feature, if not more. What are yours?

Become better acquainted with your body by answering the questions below in your clothing notebook. These answers will help you to paint a picture of what types and styles of clothing look best on your body type.

✦ What is your best body feature?
Now, learn how to show it off. If your best body feature is your chest or bustline, wear tops that play up that asset. V-neck tops are great for all bust sizes; tops that gather around the shoulders and neck are great for small-busted women.

✦ What body feature would you prefer to hide?
Know what types and styles of clothing can hide this feature but still make you look great. If you have a bigger behind, choose longer tops or wraps.

✦ What is the most flattering top you own? (Describe: V-neck, scoopneck, fitted, loose, et cetera.)

✦ What are the most flattering pants you own? (Describe: fitted, loose, waist-high, hip-high, et cetera.)

✦ What types of clothing do you feel uncomfortable in?

✦ What types of clothing do you consider fun?

✦ What types of clothing do you consider appropriate for work?

✦ In what ways do you add your personality to the clothing you wear? *("Adding accessory items" should definitely be one of your answers.)*

✦ What do you need to learn how to do in order to look great?

✦ Who is the person who most reflects the way you want to dress?

✦ My body type is:
  ❑ pear-shaped ❑ hourglass ❑ V-shaped
  ❑ straight up and down ❑ rounded

- ✦ I currently wear clothes that make me feel:
  - ❏ sexy ❏ playful ❏ conservative ❏ thin ❏ classy
  - ❏ rebellious ❏ punk ❏ bohemian ❏ uptown
  - ❏ natural ❏ trendsetting

- ✦ I want to wear clothes that make me feel:
  - ❏ sexy ❏ playful ❏ conservative ❏ thin ❏ classy
  - ❏ rebellious ❏ punk ❏ bohemian ❏ uptown
  - ❏ natural ❏ trendsetting

The most important aspect to dressing for your body type is to be comfortable in what you choose to wear. Knowing and learning what you like to wear takes time and practice. Make the commitment to embrace a new, beautiful, clothing you, then make it happen.

Remember, learning how to dress is about understanding and becoming aware of who you are and knowing your body type and what looks good on you. Matching who you are with your body type allows you to create the perfect clothing looks and outfits for you.

SUMMARY

- ✦ Select clothing styles that are right for you based on your body type.
- ✦ Choose flattering clothing styles by identifying: (1) your physical proportion, and (2) your best body features.
- ✦ Know your length proportion and width frame.
- ✦ Specialize in dressing your body specifically, and know what works for you.
- ✦ Embrace your best body features and learn to play them up.

CHAPTER 12

Dress for the Occasion

*Just around the corner in every woman's mind — is a
lovely dress, a wonderful suit, or entire costume which
make an enchanting new creature of her.*

— Wilhela Cushman

Where are you going? What are you doing today or this evening? Are you going somewhere where you will want to be noticed or are you just running errands?

The answer to these questions will determine not only what you wear for the day, an evening, or a specific event but also what you buy when you are shopping. Robin is going to an outdoor barbecue; what should she wear? She has a V-shaped body and she is definitely the Sporty Type. A vertically striped deep V-neck button-down and jeans with slide-on shoes, a preppy tote, and a sun hat is one option. Kelly has a rounded body with weight carried around the midsection. She is also the Sporty Type; what would she wear to the barbecue? A semi-fitted empire waist top with cropped jeans and mules is a good option for Kelly's body and personality type, along with the accessories that individualize and complete the outfit — great sunglasses and the perfect earrings.

Before getting dressed, always think about where you are going. What is the occasion? If you are a Socialite Type and the occasion is a fundraising luncheon, then a Prada suit with a button-down silk blouse, a pearl necklace, and of course, perfect grooming, with your hair and makeup done, fit the occasion. If you are the Rebel

Type with a straight up and down body type and you are meeting friends for a casual dinner, black leggings, motorcycle boots, a T-shirt, and a leather jacket will work.

It is always better to be overdressed than underdressed. If you are not sure how dressy an event will be, dress to look your best for that occasion and then you will be appropriately dressed. When deciding what to wear for a particular occasion, answer the following questions to help you determine the perfect outfit for the event:

✦ *What is the occasion?*

✦ *Where am I going?*

Both of these questions are obvious, but too often we go on remote control and don't ask the right questions when we're getting dressed. We go into frantic mode while trying to decide what to wear and focus on the wrong questions, like "What are other people going to wear?" and "How can I fit in or stand out?" Once you have developed your own personal style and have gained the confidence that comes with it, you will become less distracted by what other people might be wearing, and more focused on applying your own style to the occasion, whether it calls for casual, dressy, or somewhere in between. You will be more at ease with being yourself and showing off your own personal style.

✦ *Should I dress casual, dressy or somewhere in between?*

The answer to this question will be based on the answers to questions 1 and 2 above. Having a clear mental picture of what you define your casual clothing style to be or what a dressed-up you looks like helps you narrow your focus. An evening party dress for an Actress Type who has an hourglass shape could be a purple halter dress that scrunches in at the waist with a scalloped hem that is slightly below knee length. An Artist Type with a rounded body headed to the same party might wear a flowing calf-length dress with ankle strap heels and a choker that is more like an art piece with an ivory-shaped rose.

✦ *Do I want to stand out or be more conservatively dressed?*
There are times when you really want to blend in and that's all right; other times you will want to wear that great outfit you just bought. Check your mood; wear your personal best, whatever that may be when you are ready to get dressed.

✦ *How am I feeling about my body today?*
This question is important because when we're getting dressed and our inner dialogue reminds us how fat we may feel or how big our behind is, it is our signal to be gentle with ourselves. How we feel is not necessarily how we look. Negative inner dialogue comes from not selecting clothing that more appropriately fits your body type, and from not knowing how great you are before you add a stitch of clothing. By connecting to your inner beauty and specializing in dressing you, you can put this question in perspective relative to the other areas of your life. Still, sometimes our inner dialogue sends this signal that tells us to wear clothes we are most comfortable in — I call them the *tried and true outfits.*

Once you have answered these questions, you can begin to narrow down your wardrobe choices. If you are the Sporty Type, maybe khakis work great for a day out or catching up with old friends. Cargo pants with a silk top could be the choice for the Actress Type. The Classic Type may wear jeans and a turtleneck with boots to meet friends for lunch. If the event is more than casual, the Sporty Type can add a blazer to her khakis with mules. The Actress can add heels to her jeans and a designer bag. If you need to be more than casual with your appearance, black slacks are always a great choice for the Classic Type, with a tweed blazer, or even a leather jacket, if that is your own personal style. If the event is dressy, then by all means the Actress could wear a sexy cutout dress with satin pumps or a beautifully fitted suit with a sequin top. The Socialite may choose a gorgeous chiffon top and a Louis Vuitton suit, Manolo Blahnik heels, and some amazing accessory items — a vintage bag and antique earrings — to dress up her outfit. The

Rebel may choose black leather pants, a see-through sheer top with bra underneath and high heel boots. And remember the first principle — accessories make an outfit. What you choose to wear for each occasion whether it be casual, more than casual, or dressy will be based on your personality type, body type, and comfort level. (Detailed dressing examples for each personality type can be found in chapter 2.)

By thinking logically about where you are going, you can dress for the occasion and look great without all of the craziness that can go along with the process.

There are five dressing traps that can keep us from anxiety-free dressing for the occasion:

1. *Worrying about what other people will be wearing*
    It's crucial to focus on looking your best based on your own personal style. When you know the right outfit for your body type and personality, you can let yourself be creative in what you wear regardless of how other people may be dressed.

2. *Concern about fitting in or standing out*
    Will they like me? Usually concern about fitting in or standing out comes from wanting to be part of the group, wanting to be liked. I have learned that women who dress based on their own style and personality end up gaining respect from other women because they stand out as individuals. The key to this is to become comfortable with who you are and how you dress. Confidence completes your outfit more than anything else.

3. *Internal dialogue that focuses on the negative aspects of the way we look*
    As we have seen, most women experience negative internal chatter about the way they look at least some of the time. It doesn't matter if the chatter is about being too fat or too thin or too tall; about chicken legs or huge hips — it just isn't a supportive way to communicate with ourselves. When we can control our communication style,

our anxiety level decreases and we can think logically instead of emotionally when deciding what to wear.

4. *A cluttered closet*

When our closet is cluttered and disorganized, naturally we are going to experience closet trauma and have difficulty deciding — or finding! — what we want to wear. Before I got organized, I would find myself pulling clothes out of the closet that were either wrinkled, outdated, or couldn't be paired with anything else I owned. Having a clear idea of what you own facilitates pulling together outfits. For example, if you are going to be regularly attending formal dinner parties, keep several dressy outfits ready to wear. It's nice to have a choice.

5. *Not caring about the way you present yourself*

We all have down times when we may be in a less than enthusiastic mood, when it seems as if it doesn't matter what we wear. When we care more about looking good and make the effort to do so, it increases our self-esteem, and we feel better about ourselves regardless of the circumstances. Next time you are feeling blue, go back to some of the visualization suggestions in chapter 4, and remember occasions when you felt happiest about yourself and the way you looked. Try to capture that feeling now by making the effort to look good.

When you have learned how to relax and be creative about dressing for any situation, you'll find yourself with a new level of confidence and an aptitude you may not have had before. Below are the characteristics of a woman who has mastered dressing for the occasion:

✦ She knows her own personal style. She clothes herself in order to be in her power as a woman. She does not care if she fits in or stands out.

✦ She keeps her closet organized and she finds it easy to get dressed.

+ She knows how to dress to look her best for any occasion.

+ She knows how to shop to build a wardrobe and fill in the wardrobe gaps to complete her outfits.

+ She limits negative internal chatter and controls her communication style. She tells herself she looks great no matter what she ends up wearing.

+ She has a mental image of the outfits that she loves to wear for each occasion. Those outfits are tailored, clean, and ready to wear when she wants them.

+ She is you and me and all of us, if we are confident.

The key to fine-tuning your look for any particular occasion is knowing how to coordinate outfits — mixing and matching the different styles, colors, and levels of casual to dressy in your wardrobe. The principles for conscious dressing are meant to make that process easier. When you have some free time and are not rushing to dress for a real outing, go through your closet and try on clothes, pairing different items to see how they might look together. Be daring and creative, and make notes in your clothing notebook of the outfit pairings that you like.

Below are a few sample dressing ideas to get you started thinking about how to coordinate your outfits.

Casual event outfit ideas for lunch with friends or family, parties, or barbecues:

+ Sundress, strappy sandals, hoop earrings, over-the-shoulder bag

+ Jeans, mules, necklace, V-neck top, big earrings or stud earrings, leather belt, and logo handbag

+ Jeans, tank top, fitted sport jacket, straw bag, and ballet flats

+ Flowing skirt, T-shirt, jean jacket, sandals, earrings, and saddle bag

+ Sweat suit with hip tennis shoes and hair clip

+ Cropped pants, knit top, hoop earrings, casual heels, and tote

More than Casual dressing ideas for when you want to look more than casual but not really dressed up:

+ Black pants, print top, black leather jacket, sandals, hoop or stud earrings, and tote bag

+ Jean skirt, boots, vintage jacket, art deco necklace, earrings, clutch purse

+ Lightweight suit, turtleneck, strappy, sexy high heel sandals, stud earrings, and logo clutch

+ Sweater, fitted pants or black leather pants, classic belt, flat shoes, hair clip as an accessory, tote bag

+ Dress, open-toed heels or pumps, necklace and bracelet to match, small bag or tote

And for times when you really want to get dressed up, some Dressy outfit ideas:

+ Black leather pants, lacy top, open-toed high heels or black boots, crystal earrings, fur or faux fur jacket

+ Strapless, red, A-line, fitted dress, red strappy heels, red beaded clutch purse, diamond stud earrings

+ Silk minidress with spaghetti straps, matching jacket with one-button closure, sheer nylons, Mary Jane heels, long dangling earrings

+ Suit, sexy top, matching accessories (earrings, necklace, bracelets), pumps, designer bag

+ Black beaded skirt with bandeau top, vintage choker, earrings and handbag, and strappy heels

Look in your closet and take some time to think about the clothes you own. List half a dozen of your favorite pairing outfits in all three categories — casual, more than casual, and dressy — using your clothing journal. When you have outfit ideas firmly in your mind, you are able to spend more time on grooming — doing your hair and makeup — and less time scrambling to figure out what to wear. Listing clothing pairings and outfits allows you to see what you need to buy to fill in the outfit or wardrobe gaps. In your clothing journal, take the time to describe some of the clothes you would like to wear, keeping in mind all you've learned about creating a personal image of the inner you and the simple principles for conscious dressing so far. Here are examples of some ideas:

CASUAL CLOTHING OUTFIT IDEAS — I would love to wear the following: (blue) colored sweat suit, my (Christian Dior) tote bag, (Nike) tennis shoes, (hoop) earrings

MORE THAN CASUAL CLOTHING OUTFIT IDEAS — I would love to wear the following: (black) pants, my (button-down white) shirt, (black open-toed) sandals, (black dangling) earrings

DRESSY CLOTHING OUTFIT IDEAS — I would love to wear the following: (red sequined) pantsuit, my (rhinestone) heels, (clutch) purse, (matching) earrings and necklace

Dressing for the occasion is about knowing what to wear and when. It is also about knowing your comfort level. Dressing for the occasion is made easy once you have identified your personality type and defined your image. Then the range of outfits and looks comes from who you are from the inside out. Before getting dressed, always ask this one simple question: "What is the occasion?"

SUMMARY

+ Knowing what to wear is about dressing for the occasion.
+ By avoiding the five dressing traps you may decrease dressing anxiety.

✦ Learn to embody the characteristics of a woman who knows how to dress for every occasion.

✦ Practice outfit pairing in order to better coordinate outfits.

✦ Have outfit ideas firmly in your mind for each type of occasion.

CHAPTER 13

Dress from the Top Down

*No matter what size you are, you don't
have to walk around in something boxy.*

— Emme

We've learned that conscious dressing means accessorizing, going for quality over quantity in key clothing choices, making informed use of color, understanding your own body type, and knowing how to dress for any occasion. The last principle has to do with where you begin when you're putting together an outfit. People notice what you are wearing on the top part of your body first, because the first thing they see is your face. For that reason, the clothing you wear closest to your face will have the biggest impact on the overall look of your outfit. When you are seated at a dining table, people look at you from the waist up. At parties and other social events we are usually photographed from the waist up. Dressing from the top down means choosing a clothing style that accentuates your upper body and highlights your face. This is why accessory items, especially earrings and other jewelry such as necklaces or chokers, are essential: they draw attention to your facial features and position your overall clothing look.

Choose clothing that highlights your face. The other day I put on a beautifully patterned top in my signature color with jeans and boots, and I got more compliments on how great I looked than I would have if I had spent hours trying to look perfect. The top made the outfit because it highlighted my face, and people noticed how good I looked instead of just what I was wearing. This is what we want clothing to do — highlight our unique looks, make the best of our body types, and make us stand out. The right clothing item closest to the face can shape the look of a woman. Such items include blouses, T-shirts, jackets (including suit jackets), outerwear, coats, and dresses.

Choose tops that are versatile. Many styles can be paired with a jacket, blazer, or sweater to dress the outfit up or down. For example, a white button-down top with a pink V-neck sweater over it and jeans is perfect for the Sporty Type. The same white button-down top can be paired with a blue pinstripe suit and navy pumps for a completely different look.

When you dress from the top down, you will find it easier to decide on what to wear. Black pants, a pantsuit, or a skirt can be added to almost any top, so long as you choose a top that complements your body shape and fits your personality type. For example, a Rebel Type might wear a black tank top that can be matched to any bottom, with black jeans, silver stud earrings, and combat boots.

Take the following factors into account when selecting the right clothes for the upper body:

COLOR
Be sure to color coordinate when deciding what to wear.

The colors and patterns you select should complement your skin tone and hair color to create an overall look. (See chapter 10 for detailed guidelines on color-coordinating your wardrobe.) With striped tops, keep in mind how they will look on your body type. Avoid tops with horizontal lines if you are trying to look thinner; vertical stripes give the illusion of height or length. In general, wearing a single color elongates the body and makes you look thinner. Darker tops can also be flattering if you are trying to look thinner. If you choose to wear a darker top, choose a textured fabric or unique style to make the top look special, then accessorize, perhaps by adding a necklace. So what if you have a few extra pounds? Make yourself look great and show how beautiful you truly are. I have a friend who is overweight, but it doesn't stop her from wearing bright colors and great accessories that highlight her face. Recently, I saw her wearing light gray slacks with a pink V-neck sweater and a hot pink pashmina shawl wrapped around her shoulders. She added pink teardrop earrings, strappy heels, and a big dose of self-confidence to look great. She dresses better than many women I know.

CLOTHING STYLE
*The style of clothing you choose to wear
should go with your body type.*

As detailed below, the style of clothing indicates how the item is cut or tailored; for instance, V-necks, turtlenecks, and scoop necks are several distinctive styles for tops. Blazer, double-breasted, and boxy are jacket styles. Different styles flatter women with different body types.

Here are some style tips to consider regardless of body type:

✦ A V-neck is the most slenderizing of all the necklines and can be worn well by all women. If you have a longer neck, add a necklace or choker.

✦ Tops that cling to your body highlight your imperfections, so choose the fit of your clothes carefully.

✦ Lightweight thin fabrics make you look thinner; heavier fabrics add width.

✦ Avoid overdone tops with ruffles and frills unless you can carry it off. A straight up and down body type can carry it off, but the rounded body type should avoid any top with many layers of fabric that widen her frame.

✦ Adding a matching belt will make you appear taller. Only add a belt if it works for your body type.

✦ Wrinkled clothing will make you appear larger than you are. Always wear well-ironed, cared-for clothes. It will make all the difference in your self-esteem.

When shopping for tops, in general, select shirt collars that are opposite the shape of your face. Narrow, long faces can do well with round Peter Pan collars; round faces do better with square, pointed collars such as those found on button-down suit shirts. Below are the most common top styles separated by neckline:

+ V-Neck: As stated above, this style is the most slenderizing of all necklines. A green V-neck top can be paired with an amazing jade necklace, matching jade earrings, and cream slacks for a stunning outfit that makes a statement. This style works well on all body types. Women with a V-shaped body do especially well with this style, as it directs focus downward. The Actress personality type loves to stand out in V-neck tops that elongate the body and can really show off the bustline. A cream lace deep V-neck top with red fitted trousers, chandelier earrings, and open-toed red heels makes a great holiday party outfit.

+ Turtleneck: Complements most body types, but women with round or full faces or those with short necks may want to choose another style of top that is more flattering or select a lightweight fabric to reduce fullness. This is a perfect style for the Classic Type because it can be used with multiple wardrobe pieces — skirt, blazer, slacks, or suit — and look classic every time. A black turtleneck and off-white slacks, black pumps, and hoop earrings fit any business lunch for the Classic Type.

+ Scoopneck: Best for women with medium or narrow shoulders, this style minimizes the bustline and works well for women who are large-busted.

+ Peter Pan: This style has a round neckline and buttons down in the front. It is not flattering for a short neck but can be worn well by a woman with a long neck. The round style can appear to add weight to the face, creating a look of fullness.

+ Boatneck: Forms a straight line from shoulder to shoulder and works well for most body types. Women with broad shoulders may do better with a halter top. A black angora boatneck sweater paired with a sequin miniskirt in silver and white with metallic heels would look good on the straight up and down body type, especially one with narrow shoulders and a long neck because this style flatters both.

✦ Crewneck: Round collar to the neckline. Again, the round collar creates fullness, so women with round faces or short necks may want to avoid this style.

✦ Halter: This can be a very sexy style for women with broad shoulders as it focuses attention away from the shoulders and up to the face. Small to medium bust size works well with this style.

✦ Strapless: Very sexy style; can be worn on all body shapes.

✦ Gathered: Great for women with a small bust. Allows the fabric to gather at the neckline and drape over the bust, adding width. The Socialite could pair a light pink gathered top with a dark pink skirt suit, nylons, and pumps, with diamond earrings and a Chanel bag.

BUST SIZE
The size of your bust will determine what you should wear to flatter your upper body.

A top should flatter your bust regardless of size. If you are an A-cup, make sure to choose colors and styles that highlight your face. Small-busted women can wear many styles, including bandeau tops, but they may want to avoid tops that require a full bust to fill them out. Tops with breast pockets work well for small-busted women.

Generally, women who are big-busted need to wear a bra under their top, which dictates the style of tops they will wear. They may not want to wear a top with spaghetti straps unless it has a built-in bra. Larger-busted women can show cleavage if they are comfortable doing so, as in a top with a deep V-neck.

Here are some style tips for complementing bust size:

✦ A gathered neckline makes smaller breasts appear larger.

✦ For a large bust opt for V-neck tops to lengthen the neckline; avoid boatneck styles.

✦ Darker colors on top minimize the size of a large bust.

✦ Brighter colors on top are better for small-busted women.

✦ Full-busted women should avoid boxy cuts or tops with a baggy fit that will make them appear bigger all around.

✦ With small-busted women, fitted tops are a must.

ACCESSORIES
Accessory items such as necklaces, earrings, and scarves draw attention to your overall look and your face.

A great way to take the focus off your hips or behind is to play up your upper body with a beautiful necklace and dangling earrings, or a wrap or scarf such as one with a great design like those made by Burberry.

PERSONAL STYLE
Know who you are and how you want to look.

Starting with the basics, and then using the Principles for Conscious Dressing to coordinate outfits, you will learn what you like and don't like to wear. Other people may have opinions about the way you should look or dress, but you have to wear the clothing. It is better to dress for yourself, even if you make mistakes when first assembling a wardrobe. In the long run you will begin to trust your dressing instincts, and your personal style will evolve.

Now that we've identified our own unique image and learned the practical principles for dressing to perfectly express that image, it's time to make it all happen. For that, you'll need a plan.

SUMMARY

✦ What you wear closest to your face will affect your overall clothing look.

✦ Wear clothes that accentuate your upper body features and highlight your face.

✦ Keep in mind the five clothing factors when dressing the upper body.

✦ Know the considerations for choosing a great top.

✦ Use accessory items to accentuate your face and upper body.

PART III

CREATING THE PERFECT
CLOTHING PLAN

CHAPTER 14

Getting Organized Means
Finding Clothing Bliss

Women usually love what they buy,
yet hate two-thirds of what is in their closets.

— Mignon McLaughlin

As we have seen so far, the key to eliminating closet trauma and dressing to express your inner beauty is thoughtful, creative reflection — about your self-image, your feelings, your body type, the kinds of clothing that fit your image — and organization. Knowing what you own and feeling secure that your clothes are ready and available to wear without needing cleaning or altering, makes putting outfits together easy. In order to dress creatively, you need to be organized. This chapter provides some ways to get started on this important task.

Many women do not have a clear idea of what basic clothing items they need to build a workable wardrobe. For example, how many shoes are enough? For most of us, there are never enough shoes — the more the merrier! — but what shoes should you have in your wardrobe, at a minimum, to make dressing easy and flexible? What clothing and key wardrobe items should you have at a minimum to be able to put together great-looking outfits? A list of wardrobe basics is provided in chapter 15. These basics are essential for creating the foundation of a workable wardrobe, but are not enough to create a complete wardrobe. Below is a list, separated by clothing category, of items that create a complete workable wardrobe. The items in chapter 15 are included as part of this list and are wardrobe must-have items. These are simply suggested minimums: for some women the minimum is not enough, and other women can get by with less. How many clothing items you will actually need depends on how well you coordinate your outfits and how busy your work and social lives are, as well as the requirements of each. Once you create this foundation, adding additional clothing items just expands your outfit choices and styles.

✦ **SUITS:** Three, ideally: two pantsuits, one more formal for work or an evening out, one a little more casual for lunch dates, and one skirt suit. Select styles that fit your body type so that you can wear the pants or skirt separate from the jacket or use the jacket alone as a blazer over jeans. For the Sporty Type, a black suit from Anne Klein or Ann Taylor could be your dressier pantsuit and a beige pantsuit from Banana Republic could be your more casual suit. Your skirt suit can be any look depending on your needs — trendy for a fun night out or dinner party conservative. If you are the Artist Type, you might select a flowing skirt suit with a long skirt and a jacket that is more akin to an open flowing shirt paired with a matching camisole.

✦ **SWEATERS:** One black turtleneck; one cardigan; one pullover sweater, perfect over a button-down top for work or on a cold day when you are casual. For the Classic Type, a turtleneck with a tailored suit is perfect for the office and the cashmere sweater with pearls, a pair of slacks, and strappy heels will work wonders for a night out.

✦ **TOPS:** Ten to Twenty-one: one basic cotton button-down-collared shirt, two camisoles, three fun tops for evening or day, two T-shirts (short or long sleeve), two work tops (wrap top, silk or rayon blouse), two tank tops. For the Actress Type a camisole can be paired with jeans and stand-out heels for running around town. A button-down top is a wardrobe basic for all the different personality types. T-shirts work well during the day or under a suit at night.

- **JACKET:** One jean or denim jacket, one wool or other high-end blazer. A wool blazer can be paired with jeans or slacks for evening or day. If you are the Socialite Type, a Chanel jacket may be all you need to dress up any outfit. A jean jacket is a tried-and-true wardrobe must-have.

- **PANTS/JEANS:** One pair of casual pants and one pair of slacks for work or a dinner party. Not every woman wears jeans, but for some they are a wardrobe staple. Jeans are great, for example, paired with a brocade jacket and silk top for a casual day or dinner with friends. If you wear jeans, you should have at least two pairs; if you do not wear jeans, black everyday casual pants will do the trick.

- **DRESSES:** For women who prefer pants over wearing dresses, one dress may be enough. Other women love to wear dresses, so three dresses are not enough. At a minimum, one evening dress, two work dresses, and two casual or daytime dresses. If you do not typically wear dresses to the office, then add a second evening dress and sundress or even perhaps a traditional sheath dress.

- **SHOES:** One pair of pumps, one pair of evening shoes (strappy heels), one pair of casual everyday shoes (sandals), one everything casual shoe (Uggs, thongs), two pairs of boots (one casual, the other a little dressier; one or both can have heels depending on what you like to wear), one pair of tennis shoes for working out.

- **OUTERWEAR:** One raincoat, one overcoat, and one parka. Choose styles that fit your body type and, as discussed in chapter 9, choose quality or items that at least can be worn many times so that they can be paired with many outfits to create different clothing looks.

- **HANDBAGS:** Four bags; one everyday bag, one casual tote for the market or beach, one briefcase or work tote, and one evening bag. What styles, colors, and fabrics you choose will be based on your clothing personality type.

- **LINGERIE:** Lingerie is so personal; some women can never get enough of sexy underwear or G-strings, other women love comfy pajamas. How much lingerie you own is really up to you. At a minimum, three good bras are essential: one smooth for T-shirts, one racerback, and one everyday bra. Of course you can always add a sexy lace bra. Panties and sleepwear are your choice.

✦ **ACCESSORIES:** Wraps, scarves, jewelry, hats, belts, and hair accessories. How many accessory items you own will be based on how often you wear them and personal preference, including personality type. For example, a Classic Type may wear fewer accessory items than an Actress Type. The key is to know what you own and wear every item. Don't get into the habit of buying things and never wearing them.

With the above list in mind, it is important to figure out exactly what clothing items you currently own — what is the palette you have to work with in creating the perfect image of you? Here are the steps to take to get started:

1. Clean out your closet.

2. Fix up clothing and accessory items that need repair.

3. Give away what you don't wear.

Why do most of us avoid cleaning out our closets? What was your first reaction to that question? Did you just want to flip the pages and skip to another chapter? The closet for many of us is a black hole our clothes disappear into; either we can't find what we are looking for or we turn up items we never want to wear again. The closet seems to take on a life of its own, reminding us how much stuff we own, how unorganized we are, how much money we have spent on clothes and yet we still don't have anything to wear.

Cleaning out your closet and organizing your wardrobe ultimately frees you to be more creative; with your wearable clothing right in front of you and easy to find, you can more easily start experimenting with mixing and matching. When I cleaned out my closet, I found a beautiful vintage dress with orange beading I had forgotten about. After having it cleaned, I paired it with retro heels and vintage earrings, and I had a stunning new outfit for a black-tie affair.

Clothes can sometimes function like an old photograph, reminding us of times when we were especially happy, or of other times when we were not so happy. We may remember a great date or romantic evening when we come across a shirt we wore on that occasion. Or we may pick up an old pair of black pants and sigh over how much thinner we were when they still fit us.

Cleaning out your closet and taking inventory is a way to take control of your clothing personality. It is also a way to build a wardrobe that works for you now and in the future. It empowers you to decide once and for all that you own and wear your clothes — your clothes don't own you.

Cleaning out your closet is a crucial step toward simplifying the dressing process. Getting rid of clothes we don't wear simplifies the process. There are five reasons we put off cleaning out our closets and taking inventory of what we own:

✦ *Cleaning out our closets reminds us how much money we have wasted on bad clothing choices.* I have not met a woman yet that has made perfect clothing choices every time she shops.

✦ *It seems overwhelming and time consuming.* It can seem overwhelming and it is time consuming, but it is worth it. Once it is done, our clothing life will become much simpler.

✦ *We don't want to get rid of anything because we imagine we may end up wearing the clothes we never wear now at some later date.* Remember: when we clean out our closets, we make space for new and better things in our clothing life.

✦ *We don't know what to keep or what to get rid of.* Once you have a clear picture of your beauty self and understand the clothing principles, you will know what needs to go.

✦ *Clothing has memory for us and we find it hard to give up the past.* Certain items not only represent the image that we have created up until now, but also our life history. Put keepsakes in the attic, not in your wardrobe.

The end result of cleaning out your closet is a clear knowledge of what you own and where to find it when you're putting together outfits, and what you may still need to buy. I often hear women who've tackled this job say things like "I didn't know I had that shirt!" or "I couldn't believe how many pairs of black pants I own!" Our natural inclination is to just keep buying new things and pushing the old clothes to the back of the closet. When we do this, we become overwhelmed and aren't able to find anything to wear. So we end up wearing the same items over and over again — the ones at the front of the closet.

The three major benefits to cleaning out our closets are:

1. *It allows us to consciously change our clothing image and create our own personal style.* It is more difficult to change our clothing style if we keep looking at the same items we may or may not wear, still hanging in our closets. Clothes remind us of who we are or who we have been. By holding on to the old ways of being and dressing, we limit our ability to create our own personal style. By releasing things that no longer suit us, we give ourselves permission to release outdated expectations of who we have to be.

2. *An organized closet makes it easier to find the clothing we want to wear.* How do you feel when you look in your closet for something to wear? Are things easy to find? Are clothing items easy to coordinate or does your anxiety level rise because you can't find what you're looking for? Wouldn't it be nice to be able to open your closet and say, "I'm going to wear my black pants with my cream top, black mules, gold hoop earrings, and my Coach handbag," and know you'll look great?

3. *An organized wardrobe reduces excess spending.* We all impulse buy and then find that we don't have anything to wear with what we bought. If we know what we own, we

will limit the need to impulse shop for things that don't match our wardrobe.

By getting real about what we own and what we need to buy, we can release a lot of the emotional anxiety — closet trauma — of dressing. Releasing clothing that doesn't work for us anymore — that doesn't fit our current body or current self-image — allows us to focus on who we are now and who we want to be going forward. This can be very difficult.

For many women, getting rid of clothes, especially different sizes if they have had weight issues, is difficult. A compromise step that may help is to put the clothes you are no longer wearing in storage or in boxes at the back of your closet for some period of time. Make a pact with yourself that you will either go through the clothes by a certain date or give them away.

Here is how to clean out your closet:

RELEASE CLOTHING ITEMS THAT DO NOT HELP TO CREATE YOUR PERSONAL IMAGE.

+ Get rid of clothes you do not feel or look great in no matter how expensive or how comfortable they are. Remember that great outfit you bought and never wore because you felt fat every time you wore it? Get rid of it, because you will remember feeling fat every time you look at it.

+ Get rid of clothing that you never wear, including those high-end items that you may have spent a fortune on. Seeing them only makes you feel guilty. It was money wasted, but lesson learned. Get rid of it.

+ Get rid of items that look old, tattered, or outdated no matter how attached you are to those clothes. There are a few exceptions: the comfy sweatshirt or other favorite clothes you wear for lounging around the house or a quick workout; that special item, whether it is a shirt, pants, or shorts that you wear only once in a while, if it makes you feel good. Remember, you are creating your own personal image — how do you want to view yourself?

+ Get rid of items that do not fit your body type.

+ Get rid of clothes in colors that are not right for you, that make you look washed out, or that don't coordinate with other colors in your wardrobe.

The only way to bring new life to your wardrobe is to make room for new clothes that fit who you want to be. Space must be created for you to begin building a new, carefully planned wardrobe that will reflect your redefined beauty self.

UPDATE YOUR CLOSET.

+ Create a pile for any clothing items that need to be altered or repaired. For example, do you need to fix the rip in that jacket you love? Does your favorite green shirt need to have a button replaced? All of these are quick fixes that will expand and improve your wardrobe and consequently the way you look and feel. How many times have you wanted to wear a pair of pants but realized they needed altering and you had never gotten around to it?

+ Create a pile for items that need to be washed or dry-cleaned. Then wash the clothes or take them to the dry cleaners right away; don't wait.

+ Separate out the items you'll be getting rid of. All those clothes, shoes, and belts you no longer wear should be given away so that someone else may enjoy them as you have in the past, when they were right for you. Create two piles: (1) items to be given away to charity, and (2) items to be thrown away. Take your giveaway pile and donate it immediately.

If you are having a difficult time letting go of certain old clothes or clothes you don't wear because of emotional triggers, place those items in a separate pile away from the clothes you plan to keep and currently wear. Every time you look at that pile say to yourself, "Others need these more than I do."

Until you have a clear idea of what you own, it is difficult to build a wardrobe. How will you know what accessory items complement your current wardrobe unless you know what that wardrobe consists of? How many pairs of black pants do you own? For many of us, black is a staple. When I cleaned out my closet, I found that I owned six pairs of black pants — in different styles, of course, but I certainly did not need to buy more. I sorted through those pants and reduced the number to four; I figured it was a start. I also realized that I needed to add more color to my wardrobe. Black was safe — it would go with everything — but it certainly did not allow me to be creative.

CREATE AN INVENTORY OF THE CLOTHES YOU ARE KEEPING.

This will help to determine what you need to buy to complete outfits, and what you may still need to pare down — as with my black pants. This inventory, arranged by category, doesn't have to be too formal and can be written on a piece of paper or in the back of your clothing notebook. There are also software programs available for keeping track of your wardrobe items. Palm Pilot offers a software program for their handheld devices called *Wardrobe Manager.* Other software companies have similar programs available. The benefit to putting together an inventory list is that you will immediately notice gaps in your wardrobe. Over time, you will need to buy items to fill in these gaps.

Categories on your inventory list can be as simple as *pants, long sleeve tops, short sleeve tops, jackets, coats, sweaters, jeans,* and so on. Under each category, list what you own with a brief description. Make sure to include the color of the item. For example, under the heading *pants* you may have: brown tapered dress pants, camel stretch pants, and patterned brown and camel-striped pants. By putting together this kind of inventory list, you will accomplish three things:

✦ You will know what you own.

✦ You will see what you need to buy to fill in wardrobe gaps.

✦ You will begin to see a pattern for what you like to wear and buy.

While you are cleaning out your closet, you should know that there are some quick fixes for clothing items you want to keep but can't wear in their current condition.

+ Do you have extra jeans that you don't wear that much anymore? Shorten them to create capri jeans. You do not need to have them professionally tailored, unless of course you want to. These cutoffs are great to run around in and add a new dimension to your casual wardrobe.

+ Flared pants can be tailored to have the legs taken in. A great pair of pants can be saved, just by changing the shape of the legs.

+ Change the buttons on your favorite coat or jacket for a new look. Any fabric store will have buttons galore to choose from.

+ Change a long sleeve T-shirt into a short sleeve or sleeveless T-shirt just by cutting off the sleeves. This works well for an old T-shirt you haven't worn. Once you make it a tank top, you can wear it to the gym.

+ For pants you love but are a little tight in the waist, just move the latch or button slightly and see if they fit better. Any tailor or dry cleaner can do this for you in a flash or you can make this easy change yourself.

Organization is one of the major steps toward healing closet trauma and looking amazing in clothes. Sometimes not knowing what to wear is really anxiety about having too much to choose from. Buy unique items such as quality wardrobe pieces and accessories and fill in from there. Learn that being perfectly dressed is not always about having more to wear but doing more with what you have.

SUMMARY

+ Get rid of clothing that you have never worn, that does not fit your body type, or that is outdated or just plain worn out.

✦ Give away clothing items you haven't worn in six months. Unique or unusual items that you may wear at a later date are the exception.

✦ Pull out clothes to be tailored or altered, then take them in to the tailor.

✦ Make an inventory list of the clothing items that you are keeping.

✦ Use your list to identify clothing items missing from your wardrobe so you can fill in wardrobe gaps.

✦ Use quick fixes to enhance your wardrobe.

CHAPTER 15

Keep It Clothing Simple

All a woman needs to be chic is a raincoat, two suits, a pair of trousers, and a cashmere sweater.

— Hurbert de Givenchy

Too often we make dressing well more complicated than it really is. We buy clothing items that do not match our body type or the rest of our wardrobe. When you begin to consciously organize your wardrobe, buying clothes and getting dressed become much simpler. You will no longer buy clothing just because. You may still impulse shop or buy on the fly but you will now be keeping your wardrobe and your personal clothing image in mind. You will purchase clothing items to fill in the gaps in your wardrobe so that you have complete clothing looks for every occasion. Keeping it clothing simple comes from knowing what you need to wear to maximize your beauty self both inside and out.

Knowing and implementing the principles for conscious dressing presented in part II helps you keep the dressing process simple. For example, selecting a simple suit allows you to add your personal flair by choosing one that perfectly matches your body type — for a woman with a rounded figure that would be a suit with a semi-fitted jacket that is not too tight in the waist and pants that are slim, drawing attention downward away from the midsection. The Socialite might pair this with a beautifully coordinated Alexander McQueen silk blouse or the Sporty Type might choose a Banana Republic button-down-collared top. Then, add accessory items — shoes, earrings, and a handbag — to complete your outfit. *Keeping it clothing simple means choosing clothing items that are easy to mix and match with other clothing items you own.*

A uniquely patterned pink blouse can be paired with black pants, jeans, or pink pants depending on your look. A top that can be worn with different clothing items is clothing simple. By adding accessory items (earrings, handbag, the right shoes) and key wardrobe items (blazer) to any of these pairings, you can have complete outfits to wear. When you can think logically about putting together outfits, getting dressed is easy.

Once you understand that the look of your outfit will be based on (1) your clothing personality, and (2) the image you want to craft, you can purchase certain wardrobe items to help craft that image. If you are interested in a casual look and you are the Actress Type, you can wear jeans with the pink top described above, and add matching accessories: sandals or mules with earrings and a great handbag. If you need to look more dressed up and you are the Socialite Type, then wear your pink blouse, pink pants, and a designer handbag and designer shoes. If you are the Classic Type and you need to be more than casual, wear your black pants with your pink blouse, pumps, and a black blazer.

Add your personal style when choosing clothes to buy or wear. For example, look for an unusual pair of jeans to pair with other clothing items. Jeans are a basic wardrobe item that, chosen correctly, can make your outfits look creative and unusual. I recently saw a woman wearing jeans that had a pleat in the center of the pant leg. This is just one of many other standout styles of jeans. She had paired these jeans with a black turtleneck and accessory items and looked great. She stood out because she had used her creativity to choose unusual styles of simple wardrobe items. This is what keeping it clothing simple is all about.

Once again, the clothing items you choose to buy or wear should easily mix and match with other clothing items you own. This can be accomplished by following the principles I've laid out, particularly Principle Three: Color Coordinate Your Wardrobe and Principle Six: Dress from the Top Down. Here is a list of wardrobe must-haves that will make coordinating outfits easy. (Use the information in chapter 14 as a fuller basis for a workable wardrobe. The items below should be part of that list.) Unless otherwise noted, choose clothing items in your signature or secondary colors.

+ black pants (or slacks)
+ all-purpose blazer (Choose a color that will go with everything.)
+ pumps (For suits, choose black or a color that can be worn with many outfits.)
+ cardigan (in your signature or secondary color)
+ jeans (if you wear jeans)
+ fitted sweater or turtleneck (Choose what works for your body type.)
+ a great suit
+ skirt
+ boots
+ leather or all-purpose jacket
+ all-purpose earrings (hoop earrings or whatever matches your face structure)
+ perfect handbag (to wear with multiple outfits)

Once you've covered this basic wardrobe list, you can begin to add clothing items that are aligned with your clothing personality and match your body type, such as blouses, unusual key wardrobe items, funky shoes, or jackets.

Below are ten ways to keep the dressing process clothing simple:

1. Keep in mind that you are assembling a cohesive wardrobe. Think logically about what to buy and wear, then add your creative flair.

2. Keep your closet and wardrobe organized so that items remain easy to find.

3. Have outfit ideas at the ready before you get dressed for any occasion so you won't be pressed for time.

4. Have a tried-and-true outfit that you can put on to look great when you are not feeling your best.

5. Add accessory items, at least earrings and a handbag, to every outfit.

6. Don't settle for clothing seconds or what I call runner-up items (items that you buy or wear because you haven't found what you really love). Only wear clothing items you love.

7. If you are a jeans person, know that jeans go with everything. You can dress up or dress down jeans.

8. As you begin to step into a new clothing you, add flair and style through the tops you wear. Keep the bottom simple. Once you expand your clothing consciousness with tops to match your personality and body type, then you will be ready to upgrade the pants.

9. Select shoes in styles and colors that work with many outfits. For example, you should own a pair of good pumps for office wear, a pair of casual shoes such as sandals, shoes for an evening out (strappy heels, for example), boots that can be paired with many outfits, and a pair of tennis shoes. As you expand your wardrobe, of course you'll add additional shoes in any style that you really love. A suggested expanded shoe list has been included in the previous chapter.

10. Have an all-purpose pair of earrings and the perfect blazer that can be added to any outfit to complete your clothing look.

We are all striving to be able to throw an outfit together without the anxiety associated with closet trauma. Keeping it clothing simple is about building a wardrobe that is easy to manage so you can create complete clothing looks simply and look fabulous in the process.

SUMMARY

✦ Keep it clothing simple by choosing items that match your clothing personality and your comfort level.

✦ Follow the Principles for Conscious Dressing to assemble a wardrobe, then add your own personal style.

✦ Make sure that you own at least some of the basic wardrobe must-haves.

✦ Know the ten ways to keep the clothing and dressing process simple.

CHAPTER 16

Implement a Clothing Plan

Fashions fade, style is eternal.

— Yves Saint Laurent

*D**ress to Express* is intended to provide a new perspective on the dressing and image process. We've covered a lot of information toward that end in the previous fifteen chapters. Now, in order to weave it all together, you'll need to create and implement your own clothing plan.

Here are some basic steps to follow as you implement a clothing plan for the new clothing you:

1. *Understand the emotions that may have held you back from realizing your dressing potential.* How do you see yourself? Are you confident before you add a stitch of clothing? If you are not confident, it is time to become so, even if you have to fake it at first. Without confidence, the perfect clothing look cannot create the perfect clothing you.

2. *Define your image.* The magic image words you wrote in your clothing journal will help focus your attention on the image you have created up until now and the image you want to create going forward.

3. *Know your clothing personality type.* Your lifestyle will play a

big role in the clothing personality you most identify with. Knowing whether you are most comfortable standing out, fitting in, or not caring about either will determine the style of clothing you will like to wear.

4. *Identify and understand your body type.* Get a sense of the clothing styles that will work best for your particular body. What is your vertical frame? How are you proportioned upward? Is the top half of your body longer than the lower half of your body? How does that affect the style of clothing you wear? What is your body shape? Are you pear-shaped, V-shaped, or rounded? What are your best body features? Try on clothes and get a sense of what looks best on you.

5. *Pay attention to the colors in your wardrobe.* Can you identify a color pattern? Do you own a lot of pink clothing items, or blue or yellow or camel? Begin to see how your wardrobe can be color coordinated. Make sure the colors you select highlight your facial features and match your skin complexion. Do you look better in white or beige? Do you have a warm or cool complexion?

6. *Clean out your closet.* Get rid of clothing items that do not match your clothing personality or the image you have defined for yourself. Repair, tailor, and clean any clothing items that you want to keep. Give away any clothing items that no longer suit you.

7. *Take inventory by making a list of the clothing items you own.* List all clothing items and review your inventory for wardrobe gaps.

8. Understand that you are building a wardrobe that will last; you want to be able to easily mix and match clothing items. *Keep it clothing simple.*

9. *Go through your accessory items and take inventory of what you own.*

10. Once you have an idea of what clothing and accessory items you own, you can begin to *fill the gaps in your wardrobe.* Do you need an all-purpose jacket or some

hoop earrings? Do you need to add key wardrobe items to expand your outfit choices?

11. *Try on the clothing items that are on your inventory list and begin to put outfits together.* See how your wardrobe items and accessories can be coordinated to create outfits for every occasion.

12. *When you go shopping to fill in the gaps in your wardrobe, keep the shopping tips found in Appendix 1 in mind.* Accept your flaws and don't let the Five Clothing Myths become your truths.

13. *Keep your clothing emotions under control.* You have an idea of what you want to buy, so stay present and don't let yourself go on remote control — or you may find yourself in the Overachiever, Accumulator, Moderate, or Depriver clothing pattern.

14. When trying on clothes, or at any time during the day, *visualize yourself beautiful.* This form of visualization will change how you are feeling in a moment.

15. You have now cleaned out your closet, filled in some of your wardrobe gaps, and you are ready to get dressed to go out to dinner with friends. As you get dressed, *control your communication style,* making sure your internal dialogue is always positive. This will make the dressing process easy and fun.

16. *Remember to dress from the top down.* This will make getting dressed a lot easier. Pick a top you like that highlights your body type, then pair it with your tried-and-true black pants and add accessory items.

17. Now you are ready to go out. You are dressed in the perfect outfit, and you look and feel fabulous. Take a deep breath and be confident. *Step into your power as a woman and believe in how beautiful you really are.*

Now let's use these steps to implement a clothing plan for Lisa. Lisa needs to work on her confidence level. She is attractive, but many times she doesn't see herself clearly. She thinks she is fat and that clothes don't look good on her. This is because most of the clothes in her wardrobe do not appropriately fit her body type. No wonder she is frustrated with the dressing process.

Lisa's first step after recognizing that she needs to work on her confidence is to define her image. How does she see herself? What five words would she use to describe her image? After some thought, Lisa comes up with the following magic image words:

+ casual
+ comfortable
+ youthful
+ relaxed
+ fun

Lisa wants to change her image to update her look. She reviews the clothing personality types and based on the magic image words above, she fits the Sporty personality type — but she would like to update her image to be more of a combination of the Sporty and the Classic Types. The reason Lisa is interested in updating her image is that her lifestyle is changing: she has changed careers. She is leaving her job with an Internet design firm where the dress code was casual and will soon be working in a business environment for an investment banking firm. She wants to look hip and stylish in a corporate sort of way. She feels that the combination of types will allow her casual personality to come forth in a more updated look. Lisa's new magic image words are:

+ conservative
+ comfortable
+ attractive
+ classic
+ dynamic

Lisa also asked her sister to describe how she saw Lisa's image. The list of key words and how they compare are shown below:

CURRENT IMAGE	NEW IMAGE	OTHER'S VIEW
casual	conservative	attractive
comfortable	comfortable	comfortable
youthful	attractive	tailored
relaxed	classic	conservative
fun	dynamic	fun

Now that Lisa has a vision of her updated image and knows her personality type, it is time to implement that vision. The next step is for Lisa to identify her body type.

Lisa has a pear-shaped body; she is a little bigger on the bottom than she is on the top. She is also equally proportioned vertically. Dressing a pear-shaped body is about increasing the apparent size of the upper body and shoulders and minimizing the attention to the lower body. Lisa also happens to be somewhat petite in size, with narrow shoulders. To balance her body, she should be wearing tops and jackets that gather at the shoulder to add bulk; shoulder pads in jackets usually do the trick. Tops for Lisa to consider for her narrow shoulders and small bust include shawl collar, gathered collar or gathered yoke, collared tops, V-neck and boatneck tops. Heavier fabrics can add bulk to the upper body as well — a tweed or brocade jacket will flatter Lisa's upper body. The hem of the jacket should never fall mid-thigh or at the widest part of the hip. Given the fact that Lisa is petite, a fitted jacket that ends around or just below her waist will work well. As the lower part of the body gets fuller, this jacket style will help blend the clothing item on top with the item on bottom so there is no break in the visual line of the body.

Lisa believes that her best physical feature is her bustline. Her bust is small but perfectly shaped, so why not show it off with clothing styles that accentuate this physical feature, such as tops that gather at the neck and then drape across the bustline? She can also wear a dress with an empire waist, which will also flatter her body type because it is fitted on top and then flares out, hiding the width of her lower body. Tops with breast pockets are flattering for Lisa given her small bust. For her new job, she would also look good in a buttoned-down suit shirt that has a full collar focusing attention upward to the bust and face.

Next it is time to look at the best wardrobe colors for Lisa. Lisa's underlying skin tone has a lot of yellow in it. She definitely has a warm complexion. She will look great in greens, yellows, beiges, browns, a red-orange, or of course black and, depending on how it is paired, white. Looking in Lisa's closet, we see that she has a lot of the earth-toned colors — she loves browns and camel tones. Her signature color can then be brown or camel. Her color-coordinated wardrobe will look like this:

+ brown (camel)   + black
+ beige   + white
+ green   + (red-orange, or yellow)

The red-orange or yellow can be used when Lisa wants a quick color pick-me-up to brighten her wardrobe. Examples of outfit combinations for the above color-coordinated wardrobe would be: a beige pant suit with a dark brown turtleneck and dark brown pumps, perfect for the office; a brown skirt suit with a green buttoned-down suit shirt and brown boots; or black slacks with a red-orange sweater with a light red pashmina wrap and black pumps. With her image and personality type defined, her wardrobe colors chosen, and her body type clarified, Lisa is ready to clean out her closet.

Using all the information provided above to make decisions, she can now get rid of wardrobe items that no longer suit her new image. Since Lisa has combined her image type (the Sporty and Classic Types), she may not have to get rid of too much in the way of clothing. Because of her new job, she will need to add some more key wardrobe items such as suits and suit jackets. Suits are versatile and ideal for a corporate work environment but then can also be used for an evening out or lunch with friends. Lisa can buy differing suit styles and multiple blouses for differing occasions. Suits create wardrobe flexibility: just adding different tops and accessory items can change Lisa's clothing look. For example, a crisp-collared top with a fitted beige pantsuit, diamond stud earrings, Mary Jane heels, and a briefcase style bag is perfect for Lisa's new job in the corporate world and yet it combines her Sporty Type with her new Classic Type. The same pantsuit can be paired with a lace top, dangling crystal earrings, a sequin purse, and strappy shoes to work well for an evening out. For a lunch date with friends, Lisa can then wear the suit pants with a knit top in her signature camel color, hip sandals, and a bucket bag.

Next Lisa compiles a clothing and accessory inventory list, and then with her list in hand she begins to put together outfit pairings. Lisa tries on clothes in her wardrobe to see what items look good together, all the while taking into account her magic image words.

As we saw above, Lisa needs to buy some more suits — she also needs to buy some key wardrobe items such as coats, jackets, and blazers to fill wardrobe gaps she has identified. She has a lot of sporty items in her wardrobe (khakis, T-shirts) but given her new job, she will need to add suits, skirts, and blazers.

She has an idea of the wardrobe items she wants to buy, so shopping should be easy. She searches the clothing racks at a big department store and takes her selected items to the dressing room. She tries on several suits; some fit her body type and others, she now realizes, are not the right style for her body type. She is learning what works for her. She puts on a yellow suit that doesn't fit quite right and notices her inner dialogue taking over with negative chatter: "I need to lose a few pounds," "I look washed out. It's my hair color; it definitely needs to be highlighted." She catches herself in the middle of a negative thought and immediately looks in the mirror and thinks, "I am great, I look good in clothes." Now she is feeling better about herself and as she tries on another suit, a neutral color wool gabardine, before she looks in the mirror, she visualizes herself beautiful, just the way she has always wanted to look. She opens her eyes and loves the new suit she has on; it fits her body type perfectly. The jacket has built-in shoulder pads that are not overbearing but add just enough width to the upper body to balance the width of her lower body. The pants are straight legged and do not have pockets, thereby minimizing the width of her hips. The color is versatile and will be able to go with many clothing items in her wardrobe. She leaves the store happy and content with her new suit, ego intact.

She is well on her way toward healing her closet trauma and her internal dialogue is positive: "I look great." She has connected to her beauty self and is ready to show the world the clothing confident woman that she always knew she could be. She is ready for her new job. She goes out to dinner with her friends and they tell her how great she looks. Mission accomplished!

Knowing how to dress to look good and then radiating inner beauty, confidence, and a strong sense of worth is what dressing to express is all about. It's about organizing and simplifying the way you view yourself and the dressing process so that the words "What should I wear?" no longer control how you feel about the way you look and who you are inside. Using the basic steps in this chapter to implement a clothing plan will allow you to match your inner beauty to your outer beauty through image. When you can connect to your inner beauty with the way you dress, you will have found your true clothing self.

The key to looking and feeling great is knowing who you are and accepting all of you — including your flaws. We are all beautiful regardless of weight, hair color, skin color, career, or anything else external that we may feel defines us. The only thing that defines us is who we believe we are, and what makes us beautiful is what we do with that belief. Our belief in who we are determines the life we lead and the people we touch with our inner beauty. Let your belief in yourself as a beautiful, capable, dynamic woman create the life you want and deserve.

SUMMARY

+ Implement your own clothing plan using the basic steps set forth in this chapter and summarized below.

+ Understand the emotions that have held you back from realizing your dressing potential. Are you an Overachiever, an Accumulator, a Moderate, or a Depriver?

+ Define your image and decide how you want clothing to make you look.

+ Know your clothing personality type and identify your clothing comfort level.

+ Identify and understand your body type. Know how you are proportioned — length and width.

+ Color coordinate your wardrobe, choosing colors that highlight your facial features.

+ Clean out your closet and take inventory by making a list of the clothing and accessory items you own.

+ Begin to put outfits together and then fill in your wardrobe gaps with new purchases.

+ Keep it clothing simple by remembering to dress from the top down.

+ As you get dressed or at any time, visualize yourself beautiful to keep your clothing emotions and internal dialogue under control.

+ Dress to express who you are, and clothing bliss will be yours.

CONCLUSION

Dress with Passion!

Once you've worked through the Seven Secrets for Expressing the Inner You, and learned and implemented the principles of conscious dressing, you will have taken the guesswork out of dressing and shopping for clothes. With these secrets and principles in mind, it is time to enjoy yourself and the way you look. Use clothing to show off the beauty of you. Nothing ruins a great outfit more than a woman who doesn't feel great about herself. I have ruined many a great night out just because I didn't think I was dressed appropriately or doubted I looked good enough. I have tortured past boyfriends and now my husband by making them wait for hours while I changed outfits twelve times just to go out to dinner, and I know I have not been alone in this process. There are many women who know how to dress but then ruin that vision by feeling insecure or being unhappy or even angry.

I was in a café recently and I noticed a beautiful woman at another table; she had a hard angry look on her face and this in and of itself made her less attractive. Close by, I saw another woman who was not as physically beautiful by societal standards, but she was much more attractive because she looked happy and comfortable with herself, her body, and the way she looked. Both women dressed to show off their physical beauty, but the first woman had not connected to her inner beauty. She hadn't learned to let her beauty shine from the inside out.

People you encounter in life will remember if you are attractive and beautifully dressed, but they will remember you more for your personality and your charisma. They will remember you if they feel good just by being around you. Clothing should be an extension of who you we are, not the only thing that defines your beauty. Clothing is just an added bonus that helps us to express the beauty inside. The clothing you wear should complement you and make you feel good about yourself. This is what *Dress to Express* is all about — giving you the self-understanding and tools to make getting dressed simple and fun, so that you can feel good about who you are and the way you look. When you are secure in yourself, you make other people feel good. And when we believe in ourselves and the beauty that lies within, there is nothing we cannot do.

APPENDIX 1

Shopping Tips to Make You Happy

1. *Buy only things that you absolutely love!* Listen to your inner voice; if you don't love an item, no matter what the salesperson says, don't buy it. Sometimes we buy things just because the salesperson was so nice to us. You may feel guilty but remember, they don't have to wear the clothes that you buy.

2. *Buy only the items that you need to build your wardrobe.* Every woman that I have talked to about shopping noted that she had bought items on impulse. When we impulse buy, we usually end up not liking what we bought, realizing that it doesn't fit right, or finding out we have nothing to wear the item with. When you are about to impulse buy, ask the following questions: "Does this fit the image I want to create?" "Does this fit my wardrobe needs?" "Does it match my body type?" If you find a black top you love that is similar in style to one you already own ask, "Will this top enhance my wardrobe?" If the answer is no, pass on the top. You will be a lot happier you did and so will your wardrobe.

3. *Always wear or bring a bra when trying on clothes.* The right bra is essential for knowing how tops will look on you. Too often I have gone shopping without a bra and found it was hard to tell if I liked what I was trying on. This is where imagination comes into play. If you are not wearing a bra when trying on clothes, you will have to really imagine what the outfit will look like when you are all dressed up.

4. *Don't eat a big meal before trying on clothes.* This goes without saying. The quickest way to feel fat when trying on clothes is to eat a big meal beforehand. The size six pants that used to look great may fit more tightly after a big meal.

5. *When trying on clothes, see if you can view yourself in a three-way mirror. It helps to see how pants look from all angles.* Pants may look great from the front but make sure they also look great from the back. You want to look great from all angles.

6. *Don't look at numbers. Disregard clothing size no matter how you feel.* Manufacturers tinker with clothing size. A size six may fit you great from one designer and terribly from the next. Buy what you love, and what fits flatteringly, and ignore size labels.

7. *Try to buy complete outfits.* When shopping, unless you know that you have an outfit match at home for the item of clothing you are buying, try to buy matching items at the same time for complete outfits.

8. *Learn to mix it up.* Know that you can match expensive items with less expensive items for a complete outfit. (Principle Two: Good Quality Never Goes Out of Style.)

9. *Shop when you feel good about yourself and your body.* Shopping can be a lot of fun, but when you are depressed it can wreak havoc on your self-esteem. When you're feeling good, you will be more likely to buy things that you really want, rather than buying simply to cheer yourself up.

10. *Have fun.* Relax, use what you've learned, and let your clothes shopping experience be fun.

APPENDIX 2

The Seven Secrets for Expressing the Inner You

SECRET ONE: Define Your Image — and Create One

SECRET TWO: Choose Your Clothing Personality

SECRET THREE: Claim Your Confidence and Be Lifted Up

SECRET FOUR: Visualize Yourself Beautiful

SECRET FIVE: Defy the Clothing Myths

SECRET SIX: Tame Your Clothing Emotions

SECRET SEVEN: Control Your Communication Style by Connecting Your Inner and Outer Beauty

APPENDIX 3

The Six Simple Principles for Conscious Dressing

PRINCIPLE ONE: Accessories Make an Outfit

PRINCIPLE TWO: Good Quality Never Goes Out of Style

PRINCIPLE THREE: Color Coordinate Your Wardrobe

PRINCIPLE FOUR: Know Your Body

PRINCIPLE FIVE: Dress for the Occasion

PRINCIPLE SIX: Dress from the Top Down

ADDITIONAL READING

Arbetter, Lisa. *Secrets of Style: InStyle's Complete Guide to Dressing Your Best Every Day.* New York: Time, 2003.

Chopra, Deepak. *The Seven Spiritual Laws of Success.* Novato, Calif.: New World Library, 1994.

De Angelis, Barbara. *Secrets About Life Every Woman Should Know.* New York: Hyperion, 1999.

Dyer, Dr. Wayne. *Your Sacred Self.* New York: HarperCollins, 1995.

Feldon, Leah. *Does This Make Me Look Fat: The Definitive Rules for Dressing Thin for Every Height, Size and Shape.* New York: Villard Books, 2000.

France, Kim and Linette Andrea. *The Lucky Shopping Manual.* New York: Gotham Books, 2003.

Gawain, Shakti. *Creative Visualization.* Novato, Calif.: New World Library, 1997.

Hay, Louise L. *The Power Lies Within You.* Carlsbad, Calif.: Hay House, Inc., 1999.

Irons, Diane. *The World's Best-Kept Beauty Secrets.* Naperville, Ill.: Sourcebooks Inc., 1997.

Johnson, Anna. *Handbags: The Power of the Purse.* New York: Workman Publishing, 2003.

Kinsel, Brenda Reiten. *40 Over 40: 40 Things Every Woman Over 40 Needs to Know About Getting Dressed.* Berkeley: Wildcat Canyon Press, 2000.

McDowell, Colin. *Fashion Today.* New York: Phaidon, Inc., 2003.

Moran, Victoria. *Younger by the Day: A Year of Transformation for Body and Spirit.* San Francisco: HarperSanFrancisco, 2004.

Mulvaney, Jay. *Jackie: The Clothes of Camelot.* New York: St. Martin's Press, 2001.

Murphy, Dr. Joseph. *The Power of Your Subconscious Mind.* New York: Bantam Books, 1982.

Robbins, Anthony. *Unlimited Power.* New York: Ballantine, 1986.

Shinn, Florence Scovel. *The Wisdom of Florence Scovel Shinn.* New York: Fireside, 1989.

Stover, Laren. *The Bombshell Manual of Style.* New York: Hyperion, 2001.

Tobias, Tobi. *Obsessed By Dress.* Boston: Beacon Press, 2000.

INDEX

INDEX

183

  cleaning out, 67, 148–51, 164
  cluttered, as stumbling block, 129
  emotional trigger items, 149–50, 152–53
  filling in the gaps, 164–65
  inventorying, 131–32, 153, 164
  minimums of key wardrobe items needed, 146–48
  organization, 129, 145
  updating, 152, 154
  wardrobe basics (list), 159
  what to get rid of, guidelines, 151–52
closet trauma, xiii, 6, 7, 170
  internal dialogue and, 73, 75–76
clothing bliss and clothing self, 4, 9
  organization and, 145–55
  three steps for implementing, 51–52
clothing choices
  accessories, 83–97
  automatic pilot (without conscious thoughts or vision of image), 7, 78
  body type, 76, 115–23
  color-coordinated wardrobe, 11, 107–13
  dressing for the occasion, 125–33
  dressing from the top down, 135–41
  dressing traps to avoid, 128–29
  influences of parents, siblings, and friends, 5–6, 11
  key wardrobe items, 100–105
  mix and match outfits, 63–64
  movie stars, pop idols, role models, emulating, 4–5, 11–12
  past experiences that shape, 4–5, 15, 62–73, 75 (see also image)
  personality types and, 16–33, 76
  personal style, 140
  sense of self (core being), 6, 12, 16
  visualizing clothing and accessory selections, 44–45, 126, 130
clothing journal, 8, 12, 41. See also exercises
clothing plan, 163–71
  basic steps, 163–65, 171
  example of, 165–70
Coach, 85
coat and outerwear choices
  Artist, 28

blazer, 159, 160
Classic, 26
dressing from the top down and, 136
as key wardrobe pieces, 65, 101
minimum number and types needed, 147
for pear-shaped body, 167
for petite frame, 11
Rebel, 32
for rounded-shaped body, 120
Sporty, 29, 30
color, 11, 107–13, 164
  Actress, choices typical of, 110
  adding color, 108–9
  Artist, choices typical of, 27, 28
  black and white, 108
  black as staple, 24, 25, 109, 127
  bust size and, 140
  color coordination grid, 112
  complexion, cool tone, 88, 110–11
  complexion, warm tone, 11, 88, 110–11, 168
  dressing from the top down and, 136–37
  hats and complexion color, 94
  for hourglass-shaped body, 115, 119
  jewelry and complexion color, 88
  messages sent by color, 109–10
  Rebel, choices typical of, 110
  scarves and complexion color, 95
  secondary colors, 108
  "selecting your season," 111
  signature color, 107–8, 109, 111, 168
  slimming, 136–37
  sunglasses and complexion color, 89
communication style, 73–79
  closet trauma and, 73, 75
  dressing process, internal dialogue during, 74–75
  emotional patterns and, 74
  exercise, listening to your inner dialogue, 75
  inner dialogue, 45, 48, 127, 128–29, 130, 169, 170
  limited connection, 77–78
  messages sent by color, 109–10
  methods for taking control of, 78–79
  moderately connected, 76–77
  very connected, 76

ABOUT THE AUTHOR

Tracy McWilliams is a speaker and author devoted to topics that enhance the lives of women, specifically those topics related to image, beauty, and self-esteem. A graduate of the University of Southern California, Ms. McWilliams has traveled extensively and currently lives in Los Angeles and San Francisco. Visit her website at:

www.tracymcwilliams.com